ASTROLOGY FOR BEGINNERS

ASTROLOGY FOR BEGINNERS

Being the first real effort to teach Astrology a simple manner free from technicalities

Dr. B. V. RAMAN

MOTILAL BANARSIDASS INTERNATIONAL DELHI

Reprint Edition : Delhi, 2024, 2025
Twenty Sixth Edition : 1992

© MOTILAL BANARSIDASS INTERNATIONAL
All Rights Reserved

ISBN : 978-81-19394-23-4 (PB)
ISBN : 978-81-19394-99-9 (HB)

Also available at :
MOTILAL BANARSIDASS INTERNATIONAL
41 U.A. Bungalow Road, (Back Lane) Jawahar Nagar, Delhi-110007
4261/3 (Basement), Ansari Road, Darya Ganj, New Delhi-110002
203, Royapettah High Road, Mylapore, Chennai-600004
12/1A, 2nd Floor, Bankim Chatterjee Street, Kolkata - 700073

Stockist : Motilal Books Ashok Rajpath, Near Kali Mandir,
Patna-800004

No part of this book may be reproduced in any form or by any electronic or mechanical means including information storage and retrieval systems without permission in writing from the publishers, except by a reviewer who may quote brief passages in a review.

Printed in India by
MOTILAL BANARSIDASS INTERNATIONAL

Foreword

One of the earliest works on astrology by my revered father Dr. B.V. Raman, this small book covers the essentials of this ancient science in simple lucid language. The basis of casting a horoscope and hints on judgment of different aspects of human life and activity are succinctly introduced to the beginner.

I thank Mr. J.P. Jain & Mr. Abhishek Jain of M/s. Motilal Banarasidaas International for bringing out this important work of Dr. Raman attractively.

December 7, 2023

Gayatri Devi Vasudev

Preface to First Edition

I have pleasure in presenting this little book designed to give a clear and concise exposition of the essential facts of Astrology. Experience has convinced me that a book free from controversial matters is an absolute necessity to meet the growing demands of the educated public.

Whilst this little treatise, as its name implies, contains nothing that is difficult to follow, the presentation is bound to make a fascinating appeal to the advanced students as well.

It is earnestly hoped that Astrology for Beginners will be of considerable assistance to those who contemplate an initial study of Astrology. Many of the writers on the subject are far too copious-they give so many rules that the beginner becomes utterly bewildered. I have tried to avoid this. The present work by no means exhausts what is known on the subject. But yet, it will be found accurate and reliable as far as it goes, and will enable any one of average intelligence to get a good insight into Astrology.

I take credit to myself to the extent my own humble experience and practice have enabled me to present the subject in a lucid and simple manner

If a study of this book should excite a wish for further instructions on the subject, I feel myself amply rewarded.

Bangalore - 560 020 **B. V. RAMAN**
12-09-1940

Preface to Twentysixth Edition

The sale of twenty five editions of a book during the life-time of the author is a somewhat rare phenomenon in Indian conditions. This bears testimony to the large demand the books on Astrology have when the subject is presented clearly in an easy and intelligible language by experts in the line.

The present edition has been elaborated further and contains two appendices, dealing with Ayanamsa Determination and Determination of ascendant and longitudes of Bhavas according to my *"Nirayana Tables of Houses"*, thus dispensing with the need for Raphael's Tables.

I am indeed grateful to the public for the extremely cordial and encouraging reception given to this book as also my other books on Astrology.

I am thankful to the publisher for having brought out this edition in an attractive manner.

"Sri Rajeswari" **B. V. RAMAN**
Bangalore - 560 020
1st February, 1992

Introduction

In this book *Astrology for Beginners* I wish to tell something by way of introduction, about Astrology a subject to confess to an interest in which is to evoke smiles of condescension from otherwise intelligent people and run the risk of being considered an eccentric. The reader is requested to go through this introduction carefully as it enables him to appreciate what Astrology is and how it is different from the so-called occultism so often mixed up with the science of divination. Is Astrology a science? Does it deserve to be ranked among other subjects which have received the stamp of the modern scientist? Many causes have contributed to the degeneration of Astrology. Firstly, there is the impenetrable prejudice which characterises the majority of the educated public who sneer at Astrology as mere superstition and excuse themselves from any investigation of its claims on the ground that some modern scientists reject it; secondly, the springing up of a large number of quacks charging rupee one per horoscope and playing on the credulity of the masses; and thirdly, the narrow-mindedness of many of the scientists which has been greatly responsible for the present degradation of Astrology. No man is entitled to pronounce an opinion on the merits of any science unless he has devoted much time to its study and investigation.

What is science? It is knowledge coordinated, arranged and synthesised. No science is perfect and no science can be called a chimerical branch before one can claim considerable proficiency in it. Take, for instance, any science and see if it is successful cent per cent or even seventy-five per cent in its experiments, Take the percentage of cures and kills effected by doctors. A learned doctor once observed that if all the *Materia Medica* is thrown into the sea so much the worse for the fishes and so much the better for man. There is a long list of incurable diseases and the medical fraternity blinks before the fury of these diseases. Jurisprudence is a grand science. What do the bright limbs of law mean when they speak about the uncertainties of law? If law is a science, where is the room for failure of justice and prevalence of injustice? Yet some of the lawyers and doctors have the impunity to classify astrologers along with quacks, gypsies, charlatans, and swindlers. When vast sums of money are spent on such chimerical subjects as meteorology what justification can the cultured public claim for rejecting Astrology and other sciences propounded by ancient Maharishis; Astrology is holding its head so proudly under the greatest disadvantages and neglect which are extended for its vilification and it is high time that sufficient patronage is extended for its revival.

Let us examine the claims of Astrology to be ranked amongst sciences. It investigates into the influences of Time. Astrology is derived from the word *Aster*-star and *Logos*-reason or logic. It is called in Sanskrit, *Jyotisha* or the science of light.

It throws light on the dark recesses of the gloomy future. It attempts to foretell the future history of man, the fates of nations, empires, kingdoms, wars, revolutions, and other terrestrial phenomena. It tells all these things not by vague guesses or gesticulations but on the adamantine basis of pure mathematical calculations. By observation, by deduction and most important of all by induction, the astrologer has actually found a correspondence between the movements of planets and events in the life of each individual and this assertion can be tested in a comparatively brief investigation by any intelligent person.

Ancient Maharshis were past masters in every branch of knowledge. Ethnology and esoteric science were for the first time promulgated in the world by the savants of India. Messmer, Swedenburg, Havelock, Darwin, Leslie Stephen and Spencer have but caught the glimpses of the heights of knowledge attained by Patanjali, Sankara, Vatsayana and Siddhas. The Rishis had solved all problems of life which modern science with the help of its limited knowledge has been endeavouring to solve. The ancient Maharshis had a great advantage over our present-day scientists. They observed thus -*Darpanay Mithyavadaha* meaning that objects observed through glasses (telescope, etc.) reveal phenomena which they do not really represent the latter have to depend for their observations on mechanical contrivances. The ancients possessed a much more accurate, dependable and comprehensive instrument with which to observe natural phenomena -their ability to function in what might be called, to use a modern scientific term, a fourth-dimensional Consciousness-Yoga "which enabled them to note, to measure, to weigh and to classify all the facts concerning the universe without the aid of micrometers and telescopes. The super-consciousness made them aware of and able to comprehend, on the one hand, infinitesimal units of Time and Space too small to be measured by the most modern scientific instruments; and on the other hand, vast spans of years and universes-spans of years guessed at only by modern a geologist in search for the age of the Earth-universes too remote to be found even by the largest telescope.' The ancient Maharishis were never content to merely observe and catalogue facts; but unlike the present-day astronomers they applied this knowledge to the material and above all to the spiritual welfare of man.

In the Hindu philosophical system in which Astrology has its roots, the short span of life, whose problems seem beyond our ability to solve, is but a small section of our destiny and the chief value of Astrology lies in its use in determining the relationship which this life bears to the whole. The modern theory of evolution deals only with the past and fails to formulate any law for the future. It is essentially materialistic and has got absolutely nothing to say of the spirit which governs that matter and shares its future course and destiny through the series of progressive expansions or unfolding. Man's existence here, says one of the disciples of Kapila, the first evolutionist in the world, is a mere repetition and reproduction of his other previous existences. His present existence is but a link in the chain of eternal existences connecting the past with the future. In each birth, he carries one step forward the inceptive propose of his creation to its goal and consummation, until he attains the one in which the past, present and future are blended together and Time and Space are annihilated. Whether the stars actually affect human lives or they afford merely an index of events that happen as a result of forces to which stars and men are equally subject, it cannot be denied that Astrology has a place amongst the exact sciences.

The entire fabric of Astrology rests on the broad principle of evolution in Time. There is a rule in Nature and every object-mineral, vegetable, and animal-must pass under this rule through all its stages. A scientific investigation of Time gives us a clue to attempt future predictions. With Time as a function when the results deducted by a series of astronomical observations are applied, our expectation is answered. Every cause must produce an effect. This effect in turn brings forth another effect and this is borne out by experience. The Hindu astrologer believes that man's actions in this world have a long tie with his moral principles. To him, this cult seemed to conform to perfect logic. Then the vision of the transmigration of the soul and the results of his past life repeated in the present floated before him. Naturally, he went on reflecting what those results were and how far they affected, deterred, and facilitated his present life. Being guided by a series of observations and intuition he discovered that certain mathematical co-ordinates gave satisfactory answers to his queries regarding the divining of future events. Stars and planets are but manifestations of matter in space and they can be located if we know the Time. Astrology is the science which records the influence of planets on the terrestrial phenomena. In a book intended for beginners, I cannot make the introduction more exhaustive. I would refer my readers to *An Introduction to the Study of Astrology* by Prof. B. Suryanarain Rao and to my own latest book *The Influences of Planets on Human Affairs* which deals with the rationale of this subject in a more exhaustive manner.

The influences of planets on man can be conveniently classified under three headings, *viz.*, physical environment, mental peculiarities, and spiritual aspirations.

Huge dark spots, some of them many times larger than the Earth, appear on the Sun and a relationship is traced between the movements of Guru or Jupiter and convulsions of magnetic spots in the Sun. In Japan, for instance, they have now discovered that the frequency of occurrence of these spots coincides with the frequency of these eruptions. The maxima and minima of earthquakes are found to synchronise with certain relative positions of Jupiter and Saturn. Incidentally this eleven or twelve-year period of maximum solar activity automatically registers itself in the angular rings of trees, etc., and if you examine a felled tree by counting the number of these rings which are the high water-marks of the rise of the sap each year, you can not only determine the age of the tree, but more important still, you can distinguish quite clearly the extra thickness of the cell-walls which occur every eleventh year or so, indicating a year of maximum activity of the Sun's prominences. Incidentally this coincides with Jupiter's period and may be indirectly due to Jupiter's reaction on the Sun, Cohesion, adhesion, gravitation and chemical combination are universal forces. It would be unreasonable to suppose that they continuously work and yet produce no influences. An atom is the smallest conceivable particle of an element and consists of a central nucleus-the proton-surrounded by the electrons revolving round it in prescribed routes or orbits. In fact, we find that within an atom the entire solar system is repeated or reflected. Man is a compound of millions of such atoms and consequently cannot remain unaffected by changes in the solar system.

As Prof. B. Suryanarain Rao says, "careful examination reveals that men are continuously subject.ed to the influences of planetary rays. Physical conditions are nothing but the action and reaction of the solar and planetary rays upon each other and upon the objective phenomena of the earth. The integration and disintegration of rocks, the influences of atmosphere, the influences of day and night and the composition and decomposition of objects-all these are due to the solar influences."

Rains are due to the Sun and that the rains affect our crops, our health and our financial affairs cannot be denied.

All these phenomena are beautifully described in the Bhoutikasutras. Sound is the lowest form of energy. Next comes heat, then light, magnetism, electricity and other. A higher form of energy can be transformed into a lower forms of energy and vice versa. All these energies are directly derived from the solar globe. Forces are energies that are embedded in the womb of Time for purposes of creation, protection and destruction. That is why the Sanskrit scientists say that all the energies for calling into existence, keeping it alive and destroying the phenomenon are embedded in the Sun. We are influenced every second by these forces, which undergo modification in their angular positions and consequently in producing results also.

The Sun is 92 million of miles away from us. His apparent diameter is 850,000 miles. And every year the Earth receives for its sustenance 2,000th million part of the total quantity of solar energy that the Sun is radiating into space 1/200,000,000. The number of human beings is 2,000 million. Thus each man wants 1/4,000,000,000,000,000th part of solar energy for his sustenance.

This infinitesimally small quantity of solar energy can call into existence the terrestrial phenomenon and destroy it. According to *Suryasiddhanta,* Saturn is the most distant planet from the Earth and the Moon the nearest. The Sun is the soul of the universe.

No manifestation of energy can occur without the Sun's light and heat. Climate is greatly affected by the planets and climate determines the character of the vegetable and animal population of a country. The phenomena of life is entirely due to the Sun.

Man is influenced by his circumstances-monetary, social or climatic. One exposed to midday Sun feels fatigued and one sitting under the evening Sun feels refreshed. The solar ray is undergoing immense modifications every second and consequently the modifications also will be varying. Solar rays fall on the skin and affect the sense of touch. They illuminate and affect the sense of vision. They tan the skin though the effect is not cognizable by any sense. Man drinks water and is affected by it. Climatic conditions influence him. Minerals and animals affect him. And all these are governed by the Sun. Negroes have thick lips, curled hair and grotesque forms. Patagonian's are tall. In Central Africa there are dwarfs. The females of the Negritese race have got the narrowest pelvis and this fact accounts for so many still-births among them. A spacious pelvis presages giving birth to health children. All these differences are due to the adjustment of solar energies in particular form.

Mind is the resultant of breeding and birth. It is through the body and is directly under the control of the nervous system. The brain is the seat of sensation and feeling. Sensations and feelings are centered in the brain and the nerves convey the impressions through the spinal column. Active principles of propagating species depend upon the food and other factors. In the tenth month after conception, the infant is thrown out by certain internal forces and assumes a separate Individuality. At this critical moment when it takes its first breath the surroundings will have a material influence upon the future of the child. The accident of birth is not to be disposed at all. A millionaire's son by the accident of birth inherits millions while the greatest genius may not be able to acquire a decent competency. Here comes the importance of the law of continuity and Karma Theory. Unless we grant the existence of the truth of the Karma Theory, many of the inconsistencies we find in this world cannot be satisfactorily explained at all. An abuse is a bit of sound and this apparently invisible sound vibration influences the mind and offends the person. In all these cases, we see objective bodies being directly affected by subjective influences. The Moon influences the mind. Hence, on New Moon days and Full Moon days we find lunatics to be more eccentric. Hence we have the Sanskrit saying *Chandramamanaso jataa*, meaning that the Moon influences the mind. The mental currents many vibrations of heat, light, etc.- take their strength or weakness from the influences exercised by the solar rays. Vegetation affects the mind. *Satwa*, *Rajasa*, and *Tamasa* are characteristics which are due to the kind of food we take in. Man is the microcosm-*Pindanda*-corresponding with the universe or macrocosm-*Brahmanda*-and therefore we must expect to find that the vicissitudes of humanity correspond with the changes which take place in the heavens and as a consequence of which on the Earth also. The angular formations of planetary rays will be varying almost every second with the result their influences on the terrestrial phenomena must necessarily be varying. Hence we find that ever if two individuals are born at the same hour one will decidedly be different from the other.

A question that is often put with an air of derision is how can the stars be removed as they are millions and billions of miles away from us, affect affairs on the Earth? What are the means by which the stars influence us? Science is abandoning the hypothetical ether and substituting for the idea that of a magnetic field covering all space. Science knows of three fields, viz., magnetic field, electric field, and gravitational field. For the celestial bodies to affect the things of this Earth, energy from them must be transmitted. It is light-which, of course, is a form of energy, which is transmitted to us from the stars via the medium of our magnetic field. Let us for instance take the constellation of Cancer, which consists of some seven fixed stars. Stars are luminous bodies. Therefore, considering them as charged bodies radiating energy into space, it is evident that rays of light coming from the stars of this constellation must also be surrounded by their own magnetic fields. A body will not radiate energy unless there be another body within gauge to receive it. (At least the phenomenon will not be apparent.) Therefore, the fact that a body such as our Earth receives the rays of light coming from such stars is sufficient evidence of an attraction existing between the Earth and those distant stars. But our Earth is not the only body that receives energy from those stars.

In this connection, reference may be made to Einstein's recent discovery of a whole range of new realm of radiation more extensive in range than all known forms of light, heat, X-rays, cosmic rays, etc. It is a planetary wave. According to Mr. O'Neil the radiation visualised in the mathematical concept by Einstein is made up of gravitational waves, which parallel in size and frequency electromagnetic waves, but have entirely different properties. As yet, the only demonstrated property of these gravitational waves is their ability to pull planets and comets out of their courses as these bodies move around the Sun. Massive bodies like the Earth produce disturbances in the gravitational field of cosmos and these disturbances are propagated as waves and move with the speed of light. Einstein has now found rigorous proof for the existence of the waves in a single plane, such as waves in a string. The relativity theory calls for two general kinds of gravitational waves, one stationary and the other progressing of the progressing waves there are three kinds-pure longitudinal, those half longitudinal and half transverse and those pure transverse. The Earth, for example, travelling in its orbit around the Sun produces a disturbance in the gravitational field of the Sun and this disturbance is propagated in wave form. In his interview with the science Editor of *Herald Tribune*, Prof Robertson, said that the Earth's wave would have a length which would be about the same magnitude as a light year (about 600,000,000,000 miles). This wave travels through space with the same velocity as light. There would be four crests of such a gravitational earth. wave in space between us and the nearest star which is about 4 light-years away." According to Mr.: O'Neil, the gravitational waves can have any wavelength, from the smallest found in light waves, which are measured as fractional parts of a billionth of an inch, to ones far longer than any radio-wave ever produced by man, or billions of billions of miles' lengths. It seems that it is entirely possible for gravitational waves to exist which have exactly the same length as light waves, even those within the visible spectrum which we see as coloured light.

Human eyes are probably entirely blind to these gravitational waves even though they exist in as great abundance and in as great variety as light waves. Gravitational waves are entirely different from electromagnetic waves. The latter are traceable to the electrical and magnetic charges associated with particles of matter but the gravitational waves are produced by the mass characteristics of particles or large aggregation of matter. It is not known how the gravitational waves affect the astronomical world and cause the disturbance which one planet produces on another tugging it out of its orbit.

According to Mr. O'Neil's interpretation, such effects as gravitational waves produce would be produced on the mass characteristics of matter on which they impinge.

The medium in which these gravitational waves are transmitted is still a mystery, the same kind of mystery which still envelops the transmission of light. It is interesting to note that in the case of a quantum or packet of light waves pulling an electron from an atom, distance is not a factor.

It makes no difference whether the light wave comes from a nearby lamp or a star, a thousand light-years away. The effect is the same. "Frequency and not distance is the determining factor. This is an example that completely breaks down the argument that planets and stars cannot affect human beings because they are too far away. It is interesting to note also that the Moon in its travels around the Earth is also sending out disturbances in the form of these gravitational waves and these are proportional to its period of revolution around the Earth. Similar disturbances are produced by other planets in their revolution around the Sun, and those planets which have Moons are the centers for the production of local gravitational waves produced by the movements of their satellites around them. It stands to reason therefore that if a planet can affect a body of the size of the Sun, its effects upon a mechanism as delicate as the human form could be stupendous."

Thus all beings, animate and inanimate, are subject to the influence of planets and Astrology simply tells us how and when they influence, whether they are good, bad, or indifferent and how we could alleviate, Neutralize or overcome the evil influences of such planetary configurations by adopting suitable remedies as prescribed by the ancient Maharishis. By knowing the future correctly, we can avoid many pitfalls and can so create an environment that to a great extent, we can cope with the adverse circumstances or be prepared to meet them cheerfully. In this connection the student will do well to read the articles I have written in THE ASTROLOGICAL MAGAZINE on the influence of planets.

Great men believed in and practiced Astrology, Dante declared it to be the highest, the noblest, and without defect. Kepler, Lord Bacon and Dryden were skilled in this art. Flamstead, the first Astronomer-Royal, believed in Astrology for he selected an auspicious moment for the laying of the foundation. stone of Greenwich Observatory. By the contemplation of an astrological chart Newton became attracted to the study of Astrology.

To one who is unacquainted with Astrology and yet speaks or writes concerning it in an abusive and disrespectful manner, I commend the rebuke administered by Newton to Halley: "I have studied these things, you have not." In the modern times it has been the singular good fortune of late Prof. B. Suryanarain Rao, my revered grandfather, to have given a rational exposition of this abstruse science by his varied translations, original works, compilations and researches into the subject of Astrology. A knowledge of Astrology is highly essential for every individual. Fools obey the planets while wise men control them. For a fuller appreciation of the theoretical basis of Astrology, the reader is referred to Prof. B. Suryanarain Rao's *An Introduction to the Study of Astrology* and my own book *The Influences of Planets on Human Affairs*.

I may close this introduction by making a few remarks on Mundane Astrology, a branch of Astrology dealing with wars, earthquakes, inundations, etc. The effects of the planets over the affairs of nations are found to be just as powerful as they are over the life of the individual. Prof. B Suryanarain Rao predicted the Anglo-German War (of 1914) six months in advance. Zadkiels I and II were noted for their national predictions. I myself predicted the present European War nearly one year in advance in my World Prospects in 1939-40. Hitler's aggressive designs,

Mussolini's collaboration, France's collapse in 1940, the return of the Negus to Abyssinia, Japan's Far Eastern policy, the fates of Holland, Belgium, Mussolini's Fall[1], etc., have all been correctly anticipated by me and readers can get a copy of this book and test for themselves the veracity of my statement. Risking the derisive laugh, I am bold enough to say that there is enough scientific basis to warrant the study of Mundane Astrology by those in control of a National Government or to justify the introduction into national affairs of a competent Astrological Bureau to advise on future foreign entanglements. I admit that it is too much to expect, in the present state of Mundane Astrology, for this Bureau to be always right, but if it could give the Government enough insight into future complications with foreign powers that would be worth untold millions even if this supposed Bureau made only 60 per cent of correct predictions.

The day is fast approaching however when men calling themselves scientific can no longer afford to ignore a subject which offers them the very proof they are looking for-proof that everything in this universe, including man, is subject to mathematical and geometrical laws.

It is hoped that the present work which is the first of its kind to be ever written on the simpler side of Astrology by one who has been a successful exponent of the subject, will be of considerable assistance to those who seriously contemplate an initial study of the science of horoscopy.

Bangalore   **B. V. RAMAN**
12-09-1940

---

[1] Subsequent outstanding predictions include Mahatma Gandhi's assassination, Chinese invasion of India in 1962, Nixon's resignation, the Emergency in India, Mrs. Gandhi's violent end, and a host of forecasts bearing on India and international affairs. For further details, read the book "B.V. Raman-The Man and His Mission".

CONTENTS

Foreword	v
Preface to First Edition	vii
Preface to Twentysixth Edition	ix
Introduction	xi

Chapters

I	: The Essentials Explained	1
II	: Casting the Horoscope	14
III	: Hints on Judgement	22
IV	: Longevity and Death	28
V	: Personal Appearance, Character and Mind, Health and Diseases	32
VI	: Education and Financial Prospects	38
VII	: Means of Livelihood	41
VIII	: Parents, Brothers, Enemies and Debts	44
IX	: Marriage and Children	47
X	: Timing Events	52
XI	: Horary or Answering Questions	67
XII	: Transits or Gochara	72
Appendix I Ayanamsa Determinations		77
Appendix II		79

CHAPTER - I
The Essentials Explained

Basis of Astrology

THE Science of Hindu Astrology is based on the principle of evolution in time. Every cause must produce an action. The actions of every object are far-reaching, in fact, affecting the whole universe as the object itself may be regarded as a responsible being. The Hindu astrologer believes that the accumulated results of a past incarnation are brought into the present. There are moral principles which must have a long tie. Every action-physical, moral and mental-produces in its turn another action. Astrology simply indicates the results of such actions. The human ego has undergone many births previous and has still to pass through many an incarnation before it can become one with the Supreme Being. In the course of its evolution it seeks higher or lower forms of terrestrial existence, according to the good or bad deeds (Karma) of its previous birth. Planets indicate the results of our past action, viz., our future, which is divined by the Science of Astrology. Astronomy is the foundation of Astrology. Stars and planets are but manifestations of matter in space and always obey the law of gravitation. They can be located if we know the time. The actual factors employed are the planets, the signs, constellations and other celestial phenomena.[1]

---

1. Vide Hindu Predictive Astrology.

The Zodiac and the Solar System

The zodiac is a broad band in the heavens extending 9 degrees on either side of the eclipse. The ecliptic is the Sun's path. It passes exactly through the centre of the zodiac longitudinally. The zodiac is invisible to the naked eye but is only detected by watching the movements of the planets. The ecliptic is divided into 12 equal compartments, the signs of the zodiac, each being 30 degrees in extent. The solar system is headed by the Sun and consists, including himself, of the Moon, Mars, Mercury, Jupiter, Venus and Saturn, Along with these are, of course, included the shadowy planets Rahu and Ketu.

The Constellations

The ecliptic is marked by 27 constellations or stellar points. They are measured at intervals of 13-1/3 degrees of longitude from the first point of Aries along the ecliptic. It is clear, therefore, if we know the longitude of a planet, we can say in which constellation it is. According to Hindu Astrology, the zodiacal signs and constellations are identical. Each constellation is further subdivided into four quarters and each quarter is equal to 3-1/3 degrees of longitude on the ecliptic. The signs and constellations are both reckoned from the same point viz., the zero degree of longitude of Aries, that is, the *initial point of Aries is also the first point of the constellation Aswini.*

The Signs of the Zodiac

The zodiac is divided into 12 signs or Rasis of 30 degrees each. The English and Sanskrit names of the signs with their symbols are as follows:

	Sign	Its English Equivalent	Symbol	Its extent from 0 Aries
1.	Mesha	Aries	♈	0 to 30
2.	Vrishabha	Taurus	♉	30 to 60
3.	Mithuna	Gemini	♊	60 to 90

4.	Kataka	Cancer	♋	90 to 120
5.	Simha	Leo	♌	120 to 150
6.	Kanya	Virgo	♍	150 to 180
7.	Thula	Libra	♎	180 to 210
8.	Vrischika	Scorpio	♏	210 to 240
9.	Dhanus	Sagittarius	♐	240 to 270
10.	Makara	Capricorn	♑	270 to 300
11.	Kumbha	Aquarius	♒	300 to 330
12.	Meena	Pisces	♓	330 to 360

Peculiarities of the Signs

Each sign has its own peculiarities. Their application in the delineation of future events will be described in the subsequent chapters. *Aries*-Movable, odd, masculine, cruel, fiery, of short ascension, rising by hinder part. *Taurus*-Fixed, even, feminine, mild earthy, fruitful, of short ascension, rising by hinder part. *Gemini*-Common, odd, masculine, cruel, airy, barren, of short ascension, rising by the head. *Cancer*-Even, movable, feminine, mild, watery, of long ascension, rising by the hinder part and fruitful. *Leo*-fixed, odd, masculine, cruel, fiery, of long ascension, barren, rising by the head. *Virgo*-Common, even, feminine, mild, earthy, of long ascension, rising by the head. *Libra*-Movable, odd, masculine, cruel, airy, of long ascension, rising by the head. *Scorpio*-Fixed, even, feminine, mild, watery, of long ascension, rising by the head. *Sagittarius*-Common, odd, masculine, cruel, fiery, of long ascension, rising by the hinder part. *Capricorn*-Movable, even, feminine, mild, earthy, of long ascension, rising by hinder part. *Aquarius* fixed, odd, masculine, cruel, fruitful, airy, of short ascension, rising by the head. *Pisces*-Common, feminine water, even, mild, of short ascension, rising by head and hinder part.

The Planets

Hindu Astrology takes cognizance of nine *grahas* (planets), *viz.*:

Planet	English Name	Symbol
Ravi	The Sun	☉
Chandra	The Moon	☽
Kuja	Mars	♂
Budha	Mercury	☿
Guru	Jupiter	♃
Sukra	Venus	♀
Sani	Saturn	♄
Rahu	Dragon's Head	☊
Ketu	Dragon's Tail	☋

The term 'planet' used in Hindu Astrology is in the sense of a celestial body or point which has the property of attraction. Hence the Sun, a star, the Moon, a satellite of the Earth, and Rahu and Ketu, two imaginary points, of concourse of orbits of the Earth and the Moon are referred to under the somewhat forced name of planets. Uranus, Neptune, Pluto, and a host of others are considered to have no effect on human affairs. These move in the heavens with ranging velocities influenced by other forces. Each of these planets influences us according to its nature.

Planetary Nature and Indications

In this article, we are giving some of the important 'significations' of the planets. The Sun-Masculine, malefic, copper colour, philosophical tendency, royal, ego, father, sons, patrimony, self-reliance, political power, windy and bilious temperament, month, places of worship, money-lenders, gold-smith, bones, fires, coronation chambers, doctoring capacity. The Moon-Mind, mother, benefic when waxing, malefic when waning, feminine, white colour, women, seamen, pearls, gems, water, fishermen, stubbornness, romances, bath-rooms, blood, popularity, human responsibilities. Mars-Brothers, masculine, blood-red colour, malefic, refined taste, base metals, vegetation, rotten things, orators, ambassadors, military activities, commerce, aerial journeys, weaving, public speakers. Mercury-Benefic if well associated, hermaphrodite, green colour, mercantile activity, public speakers, cold nervous, intelligence. Jupiter-Masculine, benefic, bright yellow colour, devotion, progeny, truthfulness, religious fervor, philosophical wisdom, corpulence, Venus-Feminine, benefic, mixture of all colours, wife, love affairs, sensual pleasure, family bliss, harems of ill-fame, vitality. Saturn-Malefic, hermaphrodite, dark colour, stubbornness, impetuosity, demoralization, windy diseases, despondency, gambling. Rahu-Malefic, feminine, renunciation, corruption, epidemics. Ketu-Hermaphrodite, malefic, religious, sectarian principles, pride, selfishness, occultism, mendicancy.

These indications are general. Their application in particular cases will be discussed later on. Malefics are always inclined to do harm; but under certain conditions, the intensity of the mischief is tempered. Benefits, on the other hand, tend to do good; but sometimes they also become capable of doing harm. The properties of the planets given above will be helpful in making predictions. For instance, a masculine planet ruling the house of children gives, during its period, male issues. The reader should become familiar with all technicalities described here.

Relations between Planets

The subject is fully dealt with in my book Hindu Predictive Astrology. These are of two kinds, viz., permanent and temporary. A planet is said to be a friend of the other whose rays it does not counteract.

Permanent Friendship

The following is the table of permanent friendship:

Planet (Graha)	Friend (Mitra)	Neutral (Sama)	Enemy (Satru)
The Sun	Moon Mars Jupiter	Mercury	Saturn Venus

Planet (Graha)	Friend (Mitra)	Neutral (Sama)	Enemy (Satru)
The Moon	Sun Mercury	Mars Jupiter Saturn Venus	None
Mars	Jupiter Moon Sun	Saturn Venus	Mercury
Mercury	Sun Venus	Saturn Mars Venus	Moon
Jupiter	Sun Moon Mars	Saturn	Mercury Venus
Venus	Mercury Saturn	Mars Jupiter	Moon Sun
Saturn	Venus Mercury	Jupiter	Mars Moon Sun

Temporary Friendship

Planets found in the 2nd, 3rd, 4th, 10th, 11th, and 12th signs from any other planet become the latter's temporary friends. The others are its enemies.

In the diagram, for instance, take the Sun and find out his temporary relationships. Jupiter is in the 2nd. Venus and Mercury are in the 12th. The Moon and Mars are in the 3rd. Therefore, Jupiter, Venus, Moon, Mars and Mercury are the Sun's Temporary friends. Saturn alone is the Sun's enemy, temporarily.

12 Pisces	1 Aries	2 Tarus	3 Gemini
11 Aqua. Saturn			Cancer 4
10 Capri.			5 Leo
9 Sagit. Moon Mars	8 Scorpio Jupiter	7 Libra Sun	6 Virgo Mercury Venus

Mixed Relations

In order to find the strengths of planets we have to mix the temporary relations and the permanent relations. Thus a temporary enemy *plus* a permanent or natural enemy becomes a bitter enemy.

Example-In the horoscope illustrated above, the combined relationships between planets are as given in the following table:

Planet	Intimate Friend	Friend	Neutral	Enemy	Bitter Enemy
Sun	Moon Mars Jupiter	Mercury	Venus		Saturn
Moon	Sun Mercury	Jupiter Venus Saturn		Mars	
Mars	Sun Jupiter	Satrun Venus	Moon Mercury		
Mercury	Sun	Mars Jupiter	Venus Moon	Saturn	
Jupiter	Sun Moon Mars	Saturn	Mercury Venus		

Venus		Mars Jupiter	Mercury Saturn Moon Sun			
Saturn		Jupiter	Venus Mars Mercury Moon			Sun

Relations between Planets and Signs

Definite relationships exist between the planets and the signs. There are four kinds of relationships which are of particular importance, viz., Ownership, Exaltation, Debilitation and Moolatrikona.

Ownership

The Sun and the Moon own or rule Leo and Cancer respectively. Mars governs Aries and Scorpio; Mercury rules Gemini and Virgo: Jupiter owns Sagittarius and Pisces; Venus rules Taurus and Libra; Saturn is the lord of Capricorn and Aquarius. A planet situated in its own sign is rendered powerful to do good.

Exaltation

Each planet is held to be exalted when it is in a particular sign. The power to do good when in exaltation is greater than when in its own sign. The Sun, the Moon, Mars, Mercury, Jupiter, Venus, Saturn, Rahu and Ketu are said to be in deep exaltation in Aries 10°, Taurus 3, Capricorn 28°, Virgo 15°, Cancer 5°, Pisces 27°, Libra 20°, Taurus 20° and Scorpio 20° respectively. Throughout the sign ascribed, the planet is exalted but in a particular degree its exaltation is at the maximum level.

Results of Exaltation

Sun: Learned, religious, strong, placid, charitable. Moon: Rich, sedulous, a man of letters. Mars: Possessing great fervour, educated, famous, princely. Mercury: Learned, cheerful, fortunate, respected. Jupiter: Chief of men, strong, respected, given to anger, supporting a large number of men. Venus: Charitable, lives to a good old age, many qualities. Saturn Skilful, charitable, opulence, long life, loving husband. Rahu or Ketu: Wealthy.

Debilitation

The debilitation or depression points are found by adding 180° to the maximum points given above. While in a state of fall, planets give results contrary to those when in exaltation.

Moolathrikonas

These are positions similar to exaltation. Sun's Moolathrikona is Leo (0° to 20°); Moon-Taurus (4° to 20°); Mars-Arics (0° to 12°); Mercury-Virgo (16° to 20°); Jupiter-Sagittarius (0° to 10°); Venus-Libra (0° to 15°); and Saturn-Aquarius (0° to 20°).

The following table shows the relations of planets and signs:

Planet	Lord	Exalation	Debilitation	Moolathrikona
Sun	Leo	♈ 10°	♎ 10°	♌ 0° - 20°
Moon	Cancer	♉ 3	♏ 0	♉ 4 - 20
Mars	Aries			
	Scorpio	♑ 28	♋ 28	♈ 01 - 2
Mercury	Gemini			
	Virgo	♍ 15	♓ 15	♍ 16 - 20
Jupiter	Pisces			
	Sagittarius	♋ 5	♑ 5	♐ 1 - 10
Venus	Taurus			
	Libra	♓ 27	♍ 27	♎ 0 - 15
Saturn	Capricorn			
	Aquarius	♎ 20	♈ 20	♒ 0 - 20
Rahu	Leo	♉ 20	♏ 20	-
Ketu	Aquarius	♏ 20	♉ 20	-

Planetary Avasthas

Avasthas are states of existence which planets get when occupying certain positions. They are 10 in number.

Deeptha or exaltation

Good progeny, gains, respect from elders, wealth. *Swastha* or own house: Fame, position, lands, happiness. *Muditha* or a friendly house: Happiness, good temper, good wife. *Santha* or auspicious divisions: Strength and courage comfort and happiness. *Sakta* or retrogression: Courage, wealth, reputation. *Peedya* or residence in the last quarter of a sign (inauspicious subdivision): Incarceration, criminal tendencies, evil nature. *Deena* or unfriendly house: Mental worry, sickness, degradation. *Vikala* or combustion (Note: Planets very near the Sun become combust): Disease, disgrace, loss of children, Khala or debilitation: Losses, mean birth, quarrels, unpleasantness. *Bheetha* or in acceleration: Losses from various sources, torture, mean habits.

Drishti or Aspect

For a beginner it is enough to know that according to Hindu Astrology, aspects are counted from sign to sign. An aspect is good or bad according to the relation between the aspecting and the aspected body. All their location with a quarter sight, the 5th and the 9th houses with a half sight, the 4th and the 8th houses with three-quarters of a sight, and the 7th house with a full sight: Saturn, Jupiter and Mars have special aspects. Saturn powerfully aspects the 3rd and the 10th houses, Jupiter the 5th and the 9th houses, and Mars, the 4th and the 8th houses. The aspect is signified by referring to the number of signs from the signification which the aspecting planet may hold. Thus if the Sun is in Leo and Saturn in Taurus (see diagram), we say that the Sun is in the 3rd from Saturn and consequently receives the powerful aspect (3rd house aspect) of Saturn.

The opposition (7th house) aspect becomes extremely good when it is produced by Jupiter and the Moon. It is held to be good when benefics aspect each other. A planet aspecting its own house whether by the 7th house aspect or special aspect will naturally increase the signification of that house. For instance, Venus aspecting the 7th house gives a good and fair-looking wife and happiness on that account.

♓	♈	Saturn	
			Sun

We have said that Mars aspects the 4th and the 8th houses in addition to the 7th house aspect. The 4th house aspect is a square aspect and sometimes this is evil and sometimes, beneficial. For instance, if Mars is the lord of the 4th and the 9th houses, he gets special qualifications to produce good aspects (by the 4th house aspect). The significations of the aspected planet and the house are greatly enhanced. The same principle applies in the case of the 8th house aspect. Jupiter aspects the 5th and the 9th houses which, in western Astrology, are trine aspects. The results vary according to the natural and temporal dignities of the aspecting and the aspected bodies. Jupiter's aspect over any planet, as a natural benefic, is of weighty importance, apart from the fact that he may be temporarily ill-disposed.

Saturn aspects the 3rd house and the 10th house. As a natural malefic his aspects are bad. But they produce good in case Saturn acquires beneficence by temporal situations. The opposition aspect has the same power to do good or bad as conjunction, according to the nature of the planet involved.

The Twelve Houses

A house is known as Bhava in Sanskrit. The twelve houses are not necessarily coincident with the twelve signs of the zodiac. They are, in fact, variable. Each sign is always 30° in extent. But the length of a house or Bhava depends upon the time of birth and the latitude of the place of the birth.

Each of the twelve houses signifies certain important events and incidents. The following are the twelve houses and their significations:

First House: Build, body, appearance, *Second House* Family, source of death, property, vision. *Third House*: Intelligence, brothers, sisters. *Fourth House*: Vehicles, general happiness, education, mother and landed properties. *Fifth House*: Fame, children. *Sixth House*: Debts, diseases, misery, enemies. *Seventh House*: Wife or husband, tact, death. *Eighth House*: longevity, gifts, *Ninth House*: God, guru, father, travel, piety. *Tenth House*: Occupation, Karma, philosophical knowledge. *Eleventh House*: Gains. *Twelfth House*: Losses, moksha.

Kinds of Houses

The 4th, the 7th and the 10th the Kendras or angles or quadrants. The 1st, the 5th and the 9th houses are Trikonas or trines. The 2nd, the 8th and the 11th are the Panaparas or succedent house and the rest are Apoklimas or cadent houses. Planets in angles generally become fairly strong; in succedent houses slightly strong and in cadent houses, utterly weak. In trines, they become very strong.

Karakas

Each planet is supposed to be the Karaka, or indicator of certain events in life. They are:-Sun is the Karaka of father; Moon-mother; Mars-brother; Mercury-profession; Jupiter-children; Venus- wife or husband; Saturn-longevity; Rahu or Dragon's Head-maternal relations; and Ketu-paternal relations.

CHAPTER - II
Casting the Horoscope

IN this chapter we shall give the method of casting the horoscope according to the Western system (which of course corresponds to Sayana amongst us) and its reduction to the Hindu system. There is a difference of about 22 degrees between the Western and the Hindu zodiacs. That is, according to the Hindu horoscope if a planet is in 20 degrees Cancer, it will be situated in the 12th or 13th degree of Leo according to Western Astrology. Why there should be this difference is within a matter a beginner need not concern himself with. My books A Manual of Hindu Astrology and Hindu Predictive Astrology throw light on this interesting subject. The difference referred to above is called Ayanamsa or Precessional Distance. Erect a horoscope as per rules given below and subtract from the positions so obtained, the Ayanamsa for the year of birth and the Hindu horoscope needed for our purpose, is obtained. (See Appendix I for determining Ayanamsa for the year of birth.

In any[1] modern ephemeris, the longitudes of planets are generally calculated for Greenwich Mean Noon (G.M.N.) or 5-30 p.m. Indian Standard Time (I.S.T.). Therefore, if birth time is given in Local Mean Time (L.M.T.) it must be converted into its equivalent Greenwich Mean Time.

---

1 Readers can acquire Raman's Ninety-Year Ephemeris (1891 to 1980 A.D.) and Raman's Ephemeris for (1981 to 2000 A.D.) which give Sayana longitudes of planets at intervals of ten days for the Sun, Mars, Jupiter, Venus, Saturn and Rahu at intervals of 5 days of Mercury and on alternate days for the Moon.

For births west of Greenwich, add four minutes for every degree of longitude to the Local Mean Time of birth.

For births east of Greenwich, subtract four minutes for every degree of longitude from the Local Mean Time of birth.

The result is the Greenwich Mean Time of Birth.

Example

Born on 2nd November 1935, Saturday, 5-20 a.m. L.M.T. (Longitude 5 hours 10 minutes 20 secs. East and Latitude 13° North).

(15° longitudes = 1 hour time)

	H.	M.	S.
Local Mean Time of Birth =	5	20	0 A.M.
Longtiture of Place =	5	10	20 A.M
Greenwich Mean Time of birth =	0	9	40 A.M.

or 0h. 10 m. a. m. (G.M.T.)

After converting Local Mean Time of Birth into Greenwich Mean Time, the planetary longitudes for the time of birth can be easily calculated.

For this, if birth is a.m. or before noon, the difference of longitude between the previous noon and the noon of the birth date for the particular planet must be noted.

If birth is p.m. or afternoon, the difference between the noon of the birth date and the next noon must be noted.

This difference is the motion of the planet in 24 hours. From this, the proportional distance covered in the G.M.T. of birth can be easily obtained.

In the example, we have obtained the birth time as 0 hours 10 minutes am. (12-10 midnight). Since the birth has occurred before noon, the difference between the longitudes on 1st November G.M.N. and 2nd November G.M.N. must be taken. The number of hours from G.M.N. to G.M.T. of birth is 12 hours 10 minutes. Referring to Raphael's

Ephemeris (page 22) for November 1935, we get the Sun's longitude on that noon Scorpio 8 deg. 8 mins. 15 sec.

Daily motion of the Sun on 1-11-1935 = 1 deg. 4 sec., i.e., Sun's motion in 24 hours =

$$\frac{1° 0' 4'' \times 12\ hrs.\ 10m}{24\ hrs} = 31'$$

The Sun's longtitude at noon
on 1 - 11 - 1935 = 8° 8' Scorpio
Add Sun's motion in
12 hrs. 10 mts. 0° 31'
The Sun's lontitude at birth 8° 39' Scorpio

This is the Sayana (Western) position of the Sun. To obtain the Nirayana or Hindu position of the Sun, the Ayanamsa for 1935 must be deducted from the Sayana longitude.

The Sun's Sayana longtitude = 8° 39' Scorpio
Ayanamsa for 1935 = 21° 30'
Subtracting, we get the
Hindu longtitude of the Sun = 17° 9' Libra

If a planet is in retrogression, it will be mentioned so in the ephemeris. Repeating the same process with regard to all planets we get their positions thus (1) The Sun-Libra 17° 9'; (2) The Moon-Sagittarius 22° 35'; (3) Mars-Sagittarius 11° 40'; (4) Mercury- Virgo 28° 35'; (5) Jupiter-Scorpio 6° 53'; (6) Venus -Virgo 1° 45'; (7) Saturn-Aquarius 12° 2'; (8) Rahu-Sagittarius 24° 34'; and (9) Ketu-Gemini 24° 34'

Lagna or the Ascendant

Find out the Sidereal Time at G.M.N. which will be found in the first column of the ephemeris. This is given for 12 noon Greenwich Time. Add to this the Local Mean Time of birth (number of hours passed after the local noon) and also add 10 seconds per hour since noon, as this represents the difference between the Sidereal Time

(S.T.) and the Mean Time If the place of birth is east of Greenwich deduct at the rate of 10 seconds per hour for every 15 degrees of longitude (or 1 hour in time) and if the place of birth is west of Greenwich add a similar quantity. This quantity represents the Sidereal Tine at the moment of birth and when this is converted into degrees it represents what is called the R.A.M.C. of birth. Then refer to the ¹Tables of Houses for the place of birth (or for the latitude nearest to the place of birth). The Ascendant and the cusps of the 10th, 11th and 12th houses will be found marked. Considering the same illustration, we proceed thus:

	H.	M.	S.
Sidereal Time for noon preceding the birth (1-11-1935) ...	14	39	23
Number of hours passed since previous noon upto birth ...	17	20	0
Add correction between Sidereal Times and Means Time ...	0	02	53
	32	2	16
	H.	M.	S.
	32	2	16
Less correcion for the difference of time between the place of birth (East of Greenwich) and Greenwich −	0	0	52
	32	1	24

Expunging multiples of 24 we get true local Sidereal Time of birth as 8 hours 1 minute 24 seconds.

The table of houses for Madras (Lat. 13° N.) must be referred to as the latitude of Madras is nearest to the latitude of birthplace itself.

---

1 The use of The Nirayana Tables of Houses by B.V. Raman and R.V. Vaidya (in place of Raphael's) will eliminate the necessity of deducting Ayanamsa, etc., as the (Hindu) longitudes of bhavamadhyas are given for intervals of 2.5 minutes of Sidereal Time, This same example worked out according to Nirayana Tables of Houses has been given in Appendix II.

Having found the nearest time corresponding to 8 hours 1 minute 24 seconds (namely, 8 hours 0 minutes and 24 seconds under the column Side real Time) we see in the next column (10) the sign Cancer and number 28 opposite the Sidereal Time showing the 28th degree of Cancer is on the cusp of the 10th house. In the next column (11) we find Leo 29 degrees; 30 degrees Virgo in the 12th; 29 degrees 31 minutes Libra on the Ascendant or the 1st house; 29 degrees Scorpio on the 2nd; and 28 degrees Sagittarius on the 3rd. The cusps of six houses are thus obtained and adding 180 degrees to each of these, the cusps of the opposite six are ascertained Now, for example by adding 180 degrees to the cusp of the 10th house that of the 4th can be found and so on. From the Ascendant so obtained and the cusps of the houses deduct the Ayanamsa, namely, 21 degrees 30 minutes and the houses (Bhavas) and the Ascendant (Lagna) of the Hindu zodiac are obtained. Cusp of the Western House less Ayanamsa will give the Bhavamadhya (mid-point) of the house of the Hindus.

Cusp of the first house of

	Ascendant	29° 39' Libra
Less Ayanamsa for 1935		-21° 30'
Mid-point of Lagna or Ascendant		8° 1' Libra

Similarly deduct the Ayanamsa from the cusps of the other houses obtained above and you will get the corresponding Hindu Bhavamadhyas (mid-points of houses).

The Horoscope

For ordinary purposes of prediction, a zodiacal diagram (Rasi Chakra) with the Ascendant marked is sufficient. The zodiacal diagram regarding the horoscope illustrated is given below along with the Navamsa diagram which plays a unique part in Hindu Astrology. It has a great bearing on the interpretation of horoscopes.

When a sign is divided into 2 equal parts each part measuring 3° 20' is called a Navamsa. The nine Navamsas are governed by the lords of the nine signs from Aries, in the case of Aries, Leo and Sagittarius; from Capricorn in the case of Taurus, Virgo and Capricorn; from Libra in the case of Gemini, Libra and Aquarius; and in the case of Cancer, Scorpio and Pisces from Cancer. For instance, a planet is in Libra 20° 10'. This means the seventh Navamsa. In Libra the lord of the seventh Navamsa is the lord of the seventh from Libra, that is lord of Aries, viz., Mars. In Hindu Astrology constant reference is made to Navamsa positions of planets. In a way Navamsa is much more important than the usual Rasi or zodiacal diagram.

Therefore, the reader should know how to construct the Navamsa diagram.

Table of Navamsas
NAVAMSA LORDS

SIGN	1	2	3	4	5	6	7	8	9
Mesha (Aries)	- Mars	Venus	Mercury	Moon	Sun	Mercury	Venus	Mars	Jupiter
Vrishabha (Taurus)	- Saturn	Saturn	Jupiter	Mars	Venus	Mercury	Moon	Sun	Mercury
Mithuna (Gemini)	- Venus	Mars	Jupiter	Saturn	Saturn	Jupiter	Mars	Venus	Mercury
Kataka (Cancer)	- Moon	Sun	Mercury	Venus	Mars	Jupiter	Saturn	Saturn	Jupiter
Simha (Leo)	- Mars	Venus	Mercury	Moon	Sun	Mercury	Venus	Mars	Jupiter
Kanya (Virgo)	- Saturn	Saturn	Jupiter	Mars	Venus	Mercury	Moon	Sun	Mercury
Thula (Libra)	- Venus	Mars	Jupiter	Saturn	Saturn	Jupiter	Mars	Venus	Mercury
Vriischika (Scorpio)	- Moon	Sun	Mercury	Venus	Mars	Jupiter	Saturn	Saturn	Jupiter
Dhanus (Sagittarius)	- Mars	Venus	Mercury	Moon	Sun	Mercury	Venus	Mars	Jupiter
Makara (Capricorn)	- Saturn	Saturn	Jupiter	Mars	Venus	Mercury	Moon	Sun	Mercury
Kumbha (Aquarius)	- Venus	Mars	Jupiter	Saturn	Saturn	Jupiter	Mars	Venus	Mercury
Meena (Pisces)	- Moon	Sun	Mercury	Venus	Mars	Jupiter	Saturn	Saturn	Jupiter

The following are the Rasi and Navamsa diagrams in the case of the Example Horoscope.

The diagram below (Rasi) can be read thus: Lagna is Libra. Sun is in the 1st house; Jupiter in the 2nd; Moon, Mars and Rahu in the 3rd; Saturn in the 5th; Ketu in the 9th; and Mercury and Venus in the 12th. Sun and Venus are debilitated; Mercury is exalted; Saturn is in his own house; Mars and Jupiter have exchanged places. With this data before you, study the chapters.

♓	♈		Ketu	Sun	♈	Ketu	
Sat.	RASI				NAVAMSA		Mars
				Venus Sat.			
Moon Mars Rahu	Jupiter	Lagna Sun	Merc. Venus	Lagna	Rahu	Moon	Merc. Jupiter

CHAPTER - III
Hints on Judgment

PREDICTIONS can be confidently ventured provided one is well equipped with principles that determine strengths of planets and houses. In a book of this type, I wish purposely to avoid as far as possible highly technical aspects of Astrology. Six sources of strength and weakness (*Shadbalas*) should be determined for each planet in order to evaluate the worth of a horoscope properly. For the information of the reader, I shall make a passing reference to these sources of strength. They are (1) *Sthanabala:* This is the strength acquired due to residence in friendly, own and exaltation signs not only in the zodiacal diagram (Rasi Chakra) but also in the Navamsa and other subdivisions. (2) *Digbala:* Jupiter and Mercury are powerful in the Ascendant. The Sun and Mars get directional strength (Digbala) in the 10th house. Saturn is powerful in the 7th house, and Venus and the Moon become strong in the 4th house. (3) *Chestabala or Motional Strength:* The Sun and the Moon in Capricorn, Aquarius, Pisces, Aries, Taurus and Gemini constituting Uttrayana or summer solstice and Mars, Mercury, Jupiter, Venus and Saturn in retrogression or conjunction with the Full Moon get Chestabala. (4) *Kalabala or Temporal Strength:* The Moon, Mars and Saturn are powerful during the night. The Sun, Jupiter and Venus are powerful during the day. Mercury is always powerful. Malefics and benefices are powerful during dark half and bright half of the lunar month respectively. Planets in their weekdays, months and years are said to be powerful. (5) *Drukbala (Aspect Strength):* In the first chapter, a reference is made to the significance of aspects. Aspects of benefics give full Drukbala while aspects of malefics take away Drukbala. (6) *Naisargikabala:* Each planet is supposed to produce a particular measure of strength permanently irrespective of its position. The Sun, Moon, Venus, Jupiter, Mercury, Mars and Saturn are strong in descending order. The Sun is the most powerful and Saturn is the least powerful.

It is possible to measure these various sources of strength numerically. Full details are given in my book Graha and Bhava Balas which may be studied with advantage.

The judgment of a horoscope forms the most important and difficult task of an astrologer. It must be borne in mind that, at the outset no hard and fast rules can be laid down for the guidance of the reader. In order to examine a horoscope, good power of judgment is required. The strength of planets and their aspects play an important part. To start with, the astrological student may reject the whole thing as unprofitable. But patience, perseverance and experience will help him to find an easy means to arrive at the result in no time. The following rules will be found to be of much use in arriving at a conclusion. Unskilful manipulation of co-ordinates employed may lead to erroneous conclusions.

The lords of trines are always auspicious and produce good. When benefics own quadrants, they produce evil. When malefics own quadrants they produce good. The good and evil planets become more and more powerful as they are lords of the 1st, the 4th, the 7th or the 10th houses. Lords of 3, 6, 8 and 11 do evil and cause miseries. The lords of the 2nd and the 12th houses give good results if they are in conjunction with favourable planets. The lord of the 8th, if he chances to be the lord of the 1st or is in conjunction with a benefic becomes good. Rahu and Ketu produce good results when they are posited in the sign of the benefic planets. Jupiter and Venus owning quadrants become very inauspicious. Mercury as the lord of a quadrant is less malefic than Jupiter and Venus, and the Moon lesser than Mercury. Mars does not become good when he owns only the 10th house. He must own the 5th also to become thoroughly good. If the lords of Kendras (quadrants) are in conjunction with the lords of Thrikonas (trines) without being associated with the lords of other houses they become powerful in producing good results.

Each Ascendant has a key planet, Yogakaraka (Planets causing beneficial results) and Maraka (death-inflicting planets). The following table will be useful to the reader:

Table of Benefics, ETC

Lagna (Sign)	Kruras (Malefics)	Soumyas (Benefics)	Yogakarakas (Planets including prosperity)	Marakas (Death inflicting planets)
Aries	Venus Mercury Saturn	Sun Mars Jupiter	Sun	Mercury Saturn
Taurus	Moon Jupiter Venus	Sun Mars Mercury Saturn	Saturn	Jupiter Venus
Gemini	Sun Mars Jupiter	Venus Saturn	Venus Saturn	Mars Jupiter
Cancer	Mercury Venus Saturn	Mars Jupiter	Mars	Mercury Venus
Leo	Mercury Venus Saturn	Sun Mars	Mars	Mercury Venus
Virgo	Mars Moon Jupiter	Venus	Mercury Venus	Mars Jupiter
Libra	Sun Moon Jupiter	Mercury Venus Saturn	Moon Mercury Saturn	Jupiter
Scorpio	Mercury Saturn	Jupiter Sun Moon	Sun Moon	Mercury Venus Saturn

Sagittarius	Saturn Venus Mercury	Sun Mars	Sun Mars	Venus Saturn
Capricorn	Moon Mars Jupiter	Mercury Venus Saturn	Mercury Venus	Mars Jupiter
Aquarius	Jupiter Moon	Venus Mars Sun Saturn	Mars Venus	Mars
Pisces	Sun Mercury Venus Saturn	Mars Moon	Mars Jupiter Moon	Mercury Venus Saturn

Yogas

Yogas are formed when one planet or sign is related to another of the same or different kind by way of aspect or conjunction. In forming a general judgment of a horoscope, it is important to examine that the Ascendant and its lord are powerful, well associated, and have no malefic aspects. A similar examination with regard to the Moon is also essential. If the Ascendant is hemmed in between two malefics, such a combination goes under the name of Papakarthari Yoga. Benefics on either side will give rise to Subhakarthari Yoga. The former tends to subject the native to a chequered career and the latter will augment the good.

If the lords of the trines combine with the lords of the angles, with some connection with the lord of the 1st house, it leads to a Rajayoga indicating high power and authority. From the Table given on pages 30-31 it is evident that each Ascendant has certain planets which act in a dignified manner and hence called Rajayoga karakas. The proper situation of such planets in Rasi and Navamsa results in a Rajayoga.

We may make a passing reference to some of the important Yogas whose presence in a horoscope is indicative of good fortune.

Gajakesari -Position of the Moon and Jupiter in an angle from each other, RESULTS-long life fame, influential relations, general success, head of a political, social or religious organisation.

Adhiyoga-Benefics in the 6th, the 7th and the 8th house from the Moon. RESULTS-happy, foeless, high position, influential and long-lived.

Sunapha-Two or more planets (excepting the Sun) in the 2nd house from the Moon, RESULTS-one born in this Yoga will be intelligent and reputed, will occupy a high position and earns well by his own exertions.

Anapha-A combination similar to the above in the 12th house from the Moon produces this Yoga. RESULTS-enjoys worldly pleasure of every kind and possesses an unruffled temper.

Durdhura-Planets on either side of the Moon give rise to this Yoga. RESULTS-rare characteristics of self-sacrifice, good servants, wealth and conveyances.

Kemadruma-Absence of planets on either side of the Moon results in this Yoga. RESULTS-dirty habits, sinful, wicked, subservient and sorrowful.

This *Yoga* gets counteracted if there is a planet in a quadrant from the Moon.

There are any number of Yogas in relation to the Sun, in relation to the Moon, in relation to the Ascendant and in relation to the planets and so forth. To include every one of these Yogas is beyond the scope of this book. Although these Yogas override several minor influences, yet we must not lose sight of the fact that they are but one element (though a strong one) in the co-ordinates which make up the final results. In the consideration of the Yogas too, the strengths of the planets, aspects, elevations, etc., should be taken into account so as to qualify the appointment. These Yogas are explained in detail in my *Three Hundred Important Combinations*.

Mutual exchange of houses between lords of the 9th and the 10th houses goes under the name of Parivarthana Yoga. A person born in this Yoga becomes great and powerful. If the lords of the 1st and 10th interchange their houses, the native attains fame, victory and lands. The conjunction of Mars and the Moon and Jupiter and Mars go under the name of Chandramangala and Gurumangala Yoga respectively. These also indicate prowess, wisdom and good fortune in general.

One of the most important factors that distinguishes Hindu Astrology from the Western system is the consideration of these Yogas. When a horoscope is presented to a Hindu Astrologer, he scans through the whole of the diagram and tries to locate the Yogas-a correct interpretation of which will reveal the worth of a horoscope.

In examining a house, we must take into con sideration:

(1) The strength, aspect and conjunction of the lord of the house.
(2) The aspect on and the occupation of the house in question.
(3) The natural qualities of the house, of its lord and planets in it or having aspects.
(4) The influences of Yogas.

If the strength of the lord is full, there will be in general a good influence on the house.

Among the many events crowding a house, those are to be selected with which the planets are most concerned naturally for the time being.

The beneficial or auspicious nature of the aspects have to be taken under all conceivable relations, both natural and temporary. Apart from all these, the Moon, the Ascendant and the 10th house must be well disposed in good signs and Navamsas and have beneficial aspects.

CHAPTER - IV
Longevity and Death

THE span of human life can be brought under four important divisions, viz., *Balarishta* or infant mortality (death before 8 years); *Alpayu* or short life (death between 8 and 32 years); *Madhyayu* or middle life (death between 33 and 75); and *Purnayu* or full life (from 75 to 120).

Innumerable combinations are to be found in ancient works for the determination of longevity. If the Ascendant and the Ascendant lord are powerful, good longevity may be pronounced. If the Lagna, the Sun and the Moon are all afflicted then the child will have a very poor span of life.

Combination for Balarishta

(1) The Moon in the 8th house, Mars in the 7th and Rahu in the 9th cause early death of the child. (2) Situation of the Moon in an angle with malefics. (3) The Moon in the Ascendant, Mars in the 8th, the Sun in the 9th and Saturn in the 12th. (4) The Sun in the Ascendant with Saturn and Rahu and Mars in the 8th produce death of the child very early. (5) The Ascendant and the 8th from the Moon's sign being aspected by malefics.

The strong positions of Jupiter, Mercury and Venus act as antidotes for Balarishta.

According as the benefics and the lord of the Lagna are all posited in Kendras (angles), Panaparas (succeedent houses) and Apoklimas (cadent houses) the life of the native may be pronounced as long (Purnayu), Medium (Madhyayu) and short (Alpayu) respectively. If the lord of the 8th house and malefics occupy similar positions, the reverse should be predicted. Ascertain the friendship or otherwise of the following pairs :-(1) Lord of the house occupied by the Moon and that of the 8th from the Moon, (2) Lord of Lagna and that of the 8th house from the Moon and (3) Lord of the house occupied by the Sun and lord of the 8th. If they are friendly, the native will be long-lived; if inimical, short-lived; if neutral, medium life.

The 3rd and 8th are houses of longevity. Saturn is the indicator of life (Ayushkaraka). The strength of the 8th house, the 3rd house, their lords and Saturn and Ascendant will add to long life. The conjunction of the 8th lord with Saturn is also good for long life.

Death will be caused by (a) planets occupying the 2nd and the 7th houses in their period; (b) lords of the 2nd and the 7th; (c) planets in conjunction with the lords of the 2nd and the 7th; (d) if the Dasa (period of a planet owning a death house-2 and 7) does not come into operation, then death will result in the period of the most malicious planet in the horoscope or in the Dasa of the lords of the 3rd and the 8th. Saturn, when he gets the power to kill, inflicts death in preference to any other planet (see Chapter X for calculating Dasas). These relations and interrelations should be measured in the Rasi as well as in Navamsa diagrams and from the Ascendant as well as from the Moon.

Here is a Balarishta Horoscope.

Saturn	Ketu		
Jupiter	Boy born 20-11-1938 at 11:30 PM at Patna RASI		
			Lagna
	Mercury Sun Venus	Moon Rahu	Mars

At the time of birth Jupiter's minor period in his own major period was passing. Jupiter is lord of 8 and is in 7. From the Moon, Jupiter is the lord of 3 and 6. Mars aspects the 8th and lord of Ascendant is in the 4th with lord of the 2nd and the 11th. The Ascendant is aspected by lord of 8th. The child died on 8-1-1939.

Another Example

♓ Ketu	♈	Sun Merc. Sat.		♓ Lagna Ketu	♈		Mars
	Born 14-6-1884 at about 10-40 a.m. RASI		Lagna Jupiter Venus		NAVAMSA		Sun Venus Sat.
						Merc.	
		Moon	Rahu			Moon Jupit.	Rahu

In the 2nd case, Saturn's period terminates on 19-9-1940. Three benefics (Jupiter, Venus and the Moon) are in angles. But the 3rd is occupied by Rahu. Therefore middle life (33 to 75) is indicated. Saturn is lord of the 7th and 8th and occupies the 8th from the Moon. Hence he is capable of killing. The sublord Jupiter is lord of the 3rd from the Moon (both in Rasi and Navamsa) and occupies the 8th (in the Navamsa) from Lagna. Hence the person died in Saturn's major period and Jupiter's minor period on 3-8-1940, just before the close of Saturn's major period.

The end of life is judged by the planets occupying or aspecting the 8th house. When benefic planets occupy these houses you may judge that the end will be peaceful and normal and that death will take place in the midst of congenial surroundings. Contrary will be the result when the 8th house (22nd Drekkana) is afflicted. Rahu in the 8th denotes danger of long suffering, and simulated death. Saturn Produces death by chills, colds, long suffering, heart failure, etc. Mars induces death by fevers, inflammatory action and by haemorrhage, Planets in fixed signs in the 8th show death from heart, throat or excretory troubles. In cardinal signs, death will be caused due to disease of the head, stomach, kidneys or skin. In common signs, lungs, bowels and nervous system become affected. Rahu produces death by assassination. Mars by cuts, accidents, burns and effusion of blood. The nature of planets and the nature of signs should be blended together. Thus Saturn in watery signs produces drowning. How, when and where death would be caused and all other particulars relating to death are elaborately discussed in Chapter 25 of my book Hindu Predictive Astrology. In the example given above as Saturn is in the 8th from the Moon, death occurred by heart affection.

CHAPTER - V

Personal Appearance, Character and Mind, Health and Disease

THE sign rising at the time of birth and the planets situated or aspecting the Ascendant and the strength or weakness of the Ascendant lord determine the personal appearance and character of the child. The following are the effects of different signs rising at the time of birth:-
Aries: Stature middle, weak-kneed, square face, round eyes, ruddy complexion; nose and forehead full, good practicability, sociable, bad temper, sometimes slow and indolent, does not hesitate to utter falsehood. *Taurus*: Broad thighs, big face, happy in life, forgiving disposition, endures hardships, prominent eyes, obstinate, behaves like a bull, practical ability, bad temper when aroused. *Gemini*: Curled hair, black lips, skilled in interpreting other people's thoughts, an elevated nose, likes music and home-keeping, tall, slender, errect figure, arms and fingers long, quick sight, manual dexterity, shy. *Cancer*: Henpecked, fleshy neck, elevated buttocks, crooked in views, short in stature, fast in walking, fond of wealth, few sons, pale complexion, heavy gait, attached to home life, psychic or occult tenden. cies are also shown. *Leo:* Reddish eyes, large cheeks, broad face, arrogant, angry at trifles, firm-minded, tall, generous, candid, honourable. *Virgo*: Shoulders and arms drooping, truthful and kindly, limited number of issues, dark hair, good mental abilities, methodical and critical. *Libra:* Lean and frail body, fair appearance, impartial in argument, brave, merciless, body slender in youth but tends to corpulence, round face, good complexion, features regular.

Scorpio: Round loins and knees, broad and expansive eyes and a broad chest, suffers from disease in early age, will do cruel acts, self-reliance, courage, envy, endurance and executive ability. *Sagittarius*: Long face and neck big ears and nose, short stature, great strength, liberal, cheerful, enterprising, humane, good-hearted, likes physical culture and travelling. *Capricorn*: Weak in the lower limbs, good strength, indolent, vindictive, devoid of shame, prominent nose, profile, selfpossessed, humaneness absent, persistent. *Aquarius*: Generally commits sinful deeds, tall, sometimes stooping, fair looking, big buttocks, intellectual, hair dark, inclined to occult matters, forgiving temperament. *Pisces*: Symmetrical and shining body, fond of wife, learned, loses vision if Sun is afflicted, small and short limbs, indolent, reserved, diffident, and dependent.

The twelve houses of the horoscope comprehend all the significations of human life. Sidereal influences find their manifestations in terms of personal appearance, character, wealth, health, happiness, debts and diseases. No cut-and-dry rules can be laid out for evaluation of these factors as sometimes there will be contradictory forces operating for whose proper reconciliation and interpretation experience is the safest guide.

Above we have simply given the probable results of different signs becoming Ascendant. They are liable to be modified by the qualities of planets posited in or aspecting such houses. The native will correspond in his appearance to the lord of the Navamsa rising or his appearance will be similar to the strongest planet in the horoscope. Generally speaking, Jupiter, Venus, the Sun and Mars, either as lords or close to or aspecting Lagna, impart to the person their respective characteristics. *The Sun*: Adds nobleness to the figure and increases health of the constitution. *The Moon*: Indicates better proportion and greater delicacy of figure. *Mars*: Gives a fair ruddiness to the person, healthy constitution, sturdy figure and a temperament principally of heat and dryness. *Mercury*: Makes the stature proportionate, well shaped, bodily temperament chiefly hot, yellowish complexion. Jupiter: Gives a fair complexion, large eyes, dignified stature. *Venus*: Produces qualities of a nature more applicable to female beauty, softness and greater delicacy. *Saturn*: Black and curly hair, tall figure, inactive and narrow chest. In regard to the mind the Moon's position is important. The Moon in conjunction with malefics and otherwise afflicted will make the subject inclined to insanity, pessimistic and always worried, wicked, morally degraded also. To recapitulate, the affliction of the Moon and Mercury is coexistent with a quick, restless and imaginative temperament most liable to mental disturbance. It holds equally ture of the affliction of the Sun and Ascendant as regards the physical constitution. Regarding character the nature of the signs and planets rising will have a large bearing. *Movable signs* indicate executive ability, pioneering spirit, ambition and capacity to make headway against difficulties. *Fixed signs* indicate stability, patience, endurance, diplomacy. Persons born in these signs will have a fixity of purpose and determination. They make pages of history. *Common signs* indicate versatility, flexibility and lack of originality. The native will have superficial knowledge of many things but lacks persistence. If the majority of planets are in fiery signs, inspirational and ardent temperament is indicated.

Intellectual temperament is shown by the planetary majority in airy signs. Watery signs show emotional temperament and earthy signs give a practical temperament.

Example

Rahu		Moon Sat.			Sat Venus		
Lagna	Born 8-8-1912 A.D. about 7-35 p.m. RASI		Sun		NAVAMSA		Ketu
			Mars Merc. Venus	Lagna Rahu Sun			Merc. Moon
	Jupit.		Ketu		Jupit.	Mars	

1[1]. Strength of the Ascendant

Aquarius, a fixed sign, rises. Mars, Mercury, Venus and Saturn aspect Lagna. The Lagna is fairly powerful.

2. Lord of Ascendant

Lord of Lagna, Saturn, is in the 4th in conjunction with the Moon exalted and aspected by Jupiter, hence good. In Navamsa, he is debilitated but gets Neecha-bhanga or cancellation of debility. Hence he is fairly strong.

3. Lagnakaraka

Thanukaraka is the Sun. He is the lord of the 7th and is in the 6th which is good and is aspected by Saturn and Jupiter. In the Navamsa his situation is not good.

Conclusion

The first house is fairly well situated. The native will be tall, fair-looking (Mars, Venus, Mercury aspecting), with lots of hair (Saturn's aspect), and constitution not very healthy (Sun afflicted). Good character, sweet manners, patient with much endurance, of quick temper,

---

1 The method of judging a house in its various aspects and arriving at a reasonable conclusion is elucidated in my *How to Judge a Horoscope*.

forgiving and found in progressive and responsible movements.

The Ascendant and the Sun, well disposed, assure sound health. The twelve signs of the zodiac commencing from Aries in general and from the Ascendant in particular govern the twelve important organs of the human body, viz., head, face, neck, heart, stomach, waist, lower belly, sexual organs, thighs, knees, buttocks, and feet respectively. In general, such signs. as are occupied by evil planets indicate want of development of deformity in the organs they represent and those signs which are occupied by beneficial planets indicate beauty and health to the organs represented by them.

		Jupiter	Ketu
	RASI		Saturn
Lagna			Mars
Venus Rahu Merc.	Sun Moon		

If the Ascendant lord has anything to do with the 6th house or its lord, the person will have a sickly constitution. Malefics in the 6th always indicate illness. Enteric and bowel disorders are brought about by the Sun in the 6th house aspected by malefics. If the Moon is in Cancer or Scorpio in Rasi or in Navamsa and is powerfully aspected by malefics, the person suffers from diseases in the anus. Asthma is indicated by the Moon being hemmed in between Saturn and Mars and the Sun in Capricorn. Ketu, Saturn and Mars in the 6th, 7th and 8th from the Lagna give rise to consumption. The Moon in the 6th and the Ascendant hemmed in between Rahu and Saturn indicates consumption. Weak Moon in the 12th with Saturn will bring about insanity to the native. The Ascendant must be powerful and should not be connected with the 6th house or its lord in any way to give sound health.

In the example given above, the lord of the Ascendant is in the 7th being hemmed in between Ketu and Mars. The lord of the 6th is in the 12th with Rahu. From the Ascendant Ketu, Saturn and Mars are in the 6th, 7th and 8th respectively. The native died in her 25th year after suffering from consumption for nearly one year.

CHAPTER - VI

Education and Financial Prospects

EDUCATION is generally ascertained from the 4th house, its lord and the Vidyakaraka or lord of education, viz., Jupiter. The 4th house indicates intelligence, Malefics in the 4th signify broken education. Jupiter and Mercury well situated give good knowledge of men and matters. Jupiter in the 4th or the 10th gives high legal education. If the lord of the 2nd is well disposed, the person becomes a good speaker and lecturer. Mercury in an angle or Venus in the 2nd gives good knowledge in Astrology. Mars in the 2nd and Mercury in an angle make one a good mathematician or give him skill in engineering. The Sun or Mars as lord of the 2nd in conjunction with Venus or Jupiter gives proficiency in logic and mental sciences. Jupiter and Venus in angles aspected by Mercury indicate good insight into philosophical subjects. Jupiter and Venus in angles will make one a versatile genius. The lord of the 4th and Jupiter should be free from the influence of the lords of 3, 6 and 11 to indicate a sound educational career.

Look to the 5th, the 2nd, the 9th and the 11th houses for financial prospects. If a benefic be in the 2nd, particularly Jupiter, and the lord of the 2nd is in a trine or quadrant or in conjunction with beneficial lords or is in the 11th, there will be considerable wealth. Any planet in the 2nd and 11th house badly aspected and the 2nd lord in conjunction with the lords of 3, 6 and 11, or otherwise afflicted, will produce difficulty in getting money and there will be stress and even poverty. Saturn in the 2nd is indicative of reversal of fortune. Such persons, no doubt, earn a lot of money but they will lose everything. The lord of the 2nd in an angle from the Ascendant lord, or the 2nd lord being a benefic and exalted, indicates signs of good fortune and success in life. If Jupiter be the lord of the 2nd, occupies the 2nd or is in conjunction with Mars, then considerable fortune is indicated. Mercury in the 5th and the Moon and Mars in the 11th give rise to immense wealth. The lord of the Ascendant in the 2nd, lord of the 2nd in the 11th, and the lord of the 11th in the Ascendant give rise to immense wealth which will be self-earned. The source of earning should be gleaned from the situation of the 2nd lord. If, for instance, the 2nd lord is in the 9th, inheritance is shown. Legacies are shown by good planets, gain by marriages is shown by benefic planets, particularly Venus in the 7th house. The financial aspects of each horoscope are capable of being increased by giving due attention to the sources of gain, as shown by the conjunctions and aspects of planets in the various houses. Thus it happens that people rise in position and affluence through association with those whose horoscopes are in harmony with theirs. Rahu, Ketu or Saturn in the 2nd shows complications and an involved state of finance, and frequently it shows loss by fraud and imposition, many ups and downs of fortune and unexpected rises and falls.

Example:

	Ketu	Sat.		Venus			Merc. Saturn Ketu Lagna
	23-10-1883 at 10-45 ghatis after sunrise RASI		Moon Jupiter Mars		NAVAMSA		
Lagna		Rahu Venus Sun	Merc.	Sun Rahu		Mars Jupit.	Moon

In the example horoscope, the 2nd house is aspected by exalted Jupiter and the Moon. Mercury is exalted in the 10th. The Sun though debilitated in the 11th gets cancellation of debilitation. Venus is in the 11th in his own house. In the Navamsa, Mars and Jupiter (Gurumangala Yoga) are in the 2nd from the Moon. From the Ascendant Venus is exalted in the 10th. All these combinations are indicative of immense wealth. Especially in Venus period, the subject amassed a great fortune.

CHAPTER - VII
Means of Livelihood

ASTROLOGY is the science which enables a man to choose the line of least resistance and which prevents a youth of intellectual tendencies from wasting the best years of his life in drudgery at the desk or bench. Generally, the profession that one pursues is derived from a consideration of the 10th house (either from the Ascendant or from the Moon whichever is powerful) and its lord, planets in the 10th house, the dominant planet in the horoscope and the situation of the 10th lord in Navamsa. I have discussed this question exhaustively in my Hindu Predictive Astrology and Prof. B. Suryanarain Rao has made a thorough exposition of it in his immortal English translation of the Sarwartha Chintamani.

Aries, Leo and Sagittarius are fiery signs; Taurus, Virgo and Capricorn are earthy signs; Gemini, Libra and Aquarius are airy signs; and Cancer, Scorpio and Pisces are watery signs. When any of the fiery signs happen to be on the 10th house then a profession involving dealings with factories, fires, army, iron metallurgy, printing, etc., will be followed. Waterly signs in the 10th house produce sailors, navigators, admirals, inn-keepers, wine and fish mongers. Earthy signs give rise to landed properties, agriculture, cloth shop, trade, gardening, etc. Airy signs indicate orators, journalists, astrologers, and avocations connected with technical knowledge. The indications of signs get modified by the indications of planets aspecting or posited in them. The Sun denotes kings, members of the political department, ministers, magistrates, lawyers and civil servants. The Sun favourably situated in relation to the 10th house bestows professions of the above nature. The Moon rules over nurses, midwives, jewellers, dealers in pearls and precious metals, and also governmental activities. Mars produces soldiers, warriors, carpenters, mechanics, surveyors, chemists, lawyers, bankers, commanders, insurance agents and butchers. Mercury gives rise to preceptors or school masters, mathematicians, authors, printers, secretaries, booksellers, accountants and insurance agents. Jupiter makes one a priest, a lawyer, a councillor, a judge, scholar and a public man. Venus produces, artists, musicians, actors, perfumers, jewellers, wine sellers and solicitors with a keen intellect. Saturn governs different kinds of professions involving responsibility and subordination, mill hands, compositors, hawkers, factory coolies and scavengers.

If there are no planets in the 10th house, then find out the lord of the Navamsa occupied by the lord of the 10th. If such a lord be the Sun, the native will be a trader dealing with drugs, chemicals and gold. If the Moon is the lord, he will be an agriculturist, dealing in pearls, etc., and serving the feminine sex. If Mars be the lord, he will be an officer, mechanic, dealer in dangerous weapons, etc. If Mercury is the lord, he will be a writer, author, mathematician and sculptor. If Jupiter, a preceptor, priest, lawyer or a solicitor. If Venus, dealer in cattle, dressmaker, dancer, artist, etc. If Saturn, a menial and subordinate officer. If two or three planets join, appropriate blending of the influences must be made and then the nature of the calling or profession determined. Starting of one's professional career, periods of prosperity, etc., should be determined during the periods and sub-periods (see Chapter x) of planets which may have anything to do with the 10th house, its lord and planets posited in the 10th house.

The 10th house is Aquarius and it is an airy sign. Three planets are placed there. The native was a great historian, astrologer, once a lawyer and was always held to be a preceptor. He dealt with bookselling, printing and other similar trades (on account of Saturn being the lord of the 10th). Dasas of Jupiter and Saturn advanced the name and reputation of the native throughout the world and enabled him to lead a most enviable life.

Example :

	Rahu Moon	Lagna	Saturn
Mercury Jupiter Sun	RASI		
Venus		Ketu Mars	

CHAPTER - VIII
Parents, Brothers, Enemies and Debts

THE indicators of mother and father are respectively the Moon and the Sun. The 4th house rules mother and the 9th the father. The good disposition of the 4th house, its lord, and the Karaka are important for getting a good and long-lived mother. The same argument applies in the case of the father. Malefics in the 4th and the 9th certainly affect the planets. The Sun afflicted brings trouble to the father and through him to the native. This may indicate a cold severe father. The presence of the Sun in the 9th with Saturn indicates early death of the father. Likewise, the presence of Saturn in the 4th with the Moon denotes early death to the mother. Afflictions to the luminaries (i.e., the Sun and the Moon) from Mars threaten the parents with accidents. The parent's affairs may, to a large extent, be judged by taking the appropriate house as the first, and then proceeding thus. The financial affairs of the father, for instance, can be judged by studying the 2nd from the 9th, his ills, the 6th from the 9th, his profession, the 10th from the 9th and so on.

If Saturn owning 9th house occupies a moveable sign and be unaspected by benefics, the child concerned lives under the care of a foster-father. If the 9th house or its lord being in a moveable sign is occupied or aspected by Saturn and if the lord of the 11th house be strong the child born is sure to be adopted by another.

The third house rules brothers and Mars is the Karaka (indicator of brothers). The 11th rules sisters. The presence of Mars in the 3rd does not indicate many brothers. The good or bad disposition (by way of aspect, conjunction, ownership, etc.) of the 3rd, its lord and Mars determines the number of brothers, their fortune, etc. The number of brothers may be ascertained from the number of Navamsas gained by the lord of the 3rd or by Mars whichever is stronger.

The 6th house governs enemies and debts. Presence of malefics in the 6th gives success over enemies and redemption from debts. If the 6th house is not occupied by any planet, either good or bad, such a combination suggests absence of enemies. If the lord of the Ascendant joins the 6th aspected by the lord of the 6th, the person will suffer much from the machinations of cousins and enemies. If the lord of the 4th is in conjunction with the lord of the 8th then the native is likely to be charged for criminal offencess. If the lord of the 11th be in good relation with the lord of the Ascendant, it shows harmonious relationships with friends.

Debts will be incurred either during the periods (Dasas) or sub-periods (Bhuktis) of planets ruling the 6th, the 8th and the 12th or of those planets who may be in conjunction with or aspected by the lords of the 6th, the 8th and (or) the 12th.

Example:

Ketu	Sun Merc. Sat.		Birth Ketu			Mars
	4-6-1884 at 11-40 ghatis at Mysore RASI	Birth Moon Venus Jupiter		NAVAMSA		Sun Venus Satrun
		Mars	Mercury			
		Rahu			Moon Jupit.	Rahu

Parents

The lord of father (Sun) is in an enemy's house in conjunction with Saturn who, besides being a natural enemy of the Sun, is also lord of the 8th. Ketu is in the 9th house and the 9th lord is in conjunction with the 11th lord and again aspected by Saturn. Father died early in life. The lord of the 4th is in Lagna in conjunction with exalted Jupiter and aspected by Saturn, a natural friend. The Moon, lord of the mother. is free from afflictions. Mother lived till about the 47th year of the native.

Brother

Mars, lord of the brothers, is in the 2nd. The 3rd house lord Mercury is in conjunction with the Sun and Saturn. The lord of the 3rd has passed one Navamsa. Hence the native had only one brother who died just a few months before the native's own death.

Debts and Enemies

The lord of the 6th is also the lord of the 9th and is in exaltation. The 6th is free from occupation or aspect of any planet-good or bad. No debts or enemies. Rolled in wealth.

CHAPTER - IX
Marriage and Children

THE study of Astrology throws a flood of light on the important question of matrimonial felicity or infelicity. Incompatibility of temperament is often alleged to be the cause of separation of married couples. By means of this science such incompatibility should be discovered before the knot is tied.

In judging the affairs of marriage, consideration should be bestowed upon Venus as he is lord of the wife or husband (Kalatrakaraka) and the 7th house and the lord of the 7th. The Sun in the 7th house gives a proud, firm-minded partner. There will be delays in marriage. The Moon, kind and domesticated partner with a wavering mind. Mars, a quarrelsome domineering wife or husband. Likelihood of frequent separation by quarrels and misunderstandings. Mercury, a quick-minded, and a bad-tempered (if afflicted) partner. Jupiter, a good wife or husband and, in general, a happy marriage. Venus, the marriage is likely to be happy if Venus is not afflicted. Otherwise, always quarrels. The native becomes highly attracted towards the opposite sex. Saturn, difference of age or status between native and partner. Generally an unhappy married life. Rahu and Ketu give tragic conditions.

The lord of the 7th should not occupy the 6th, or the 8th and the 2nd should not be aspected by malefics to assure marital happiness. If the 7th house is hemmed in between two malefics (Papakarthari Yoga), then married life proves burden-some and miserable.

If Venus be afflicted by Mars, we are likely to find tumultous feelings and little emotional calm or happiness with prolonged separation. Bad aspects between the 5th and the 7th lords may denote lifelong celibacy. If the Sun and Rahu be in the 7th house, it denotes loss of wealth through the association of women. If malefics should occupy the 4th, the 7th and the 12th houses, one will be bereft of wife and children. If the lord of the Ascendant be in the 7th subject to benefic influence, the native gets a wife or husband from a respectable family. If the Moon be in the Ascendant or in the 7th and Leo be rising in Navamsa, then the character of the native's wife becomes questionable, Venus well disposed in the 7th denotes good fortune after marriage and the enjoyment of all the fruits of married life.

In a woman's horoscope, the 8th house plays significant part. Malefics in the 8th particularly Mars bring about early widowhood. Saturn in the 8th makes the married life unromantic and charmless. When the Moon along with Saturn occupies the 7th house, the woman concerned will have more than one marriage.

If the 7th house happens to be a common sign Dwiswabhava Rasi) and Venus is there in conjunction with malefics, more than one marriage is invariably indicated.

If the lord of the Ascendant and that of the 7th are close to each other, marriage takes place early in life, A similar result may be predicted if benefics are posited in the Ascendant, the 2nd and the 7th. Marriage may occur during the Dasa (period) of the planet (1) posited in the 7th house; (2) Venus and the Moon; (3) planet aspecting the 7th house; or (4) owning the 7th house.

Issues

The 5th house rules children. Jupiter indicates progeny and the 5th lord is also connected with issues.

Favourable disposition of all these three factors is a great asset for getting good, long-lived and obedient children. If the 5th house (either from the Ascendant or from the Moon) be occupied by benefic planets well aspected by others, then the children will be a source of happiness to the subject, and they will live long. When the 5th house is occupied by malefic planets or has other heavy afflictions, opposite results will be produced. Illustrious children are born when the ruler of the 5th house is in elevation, well aspected and in a congenial sign. When malefic planets are in the 12th in a female's horoscope, there are dangers in confinement.

No children should be predicted if Jupiter, the Ascendant lord and lords of the 7th and the 5th are weak and otherwise afflicted. If Saturn be in the 5th house and the lord of the 5th be in conjunction with Rahu, the native will have no surviving children. If the 5th house and its lord be placed in a male sign or be in conjunction with or aspected by male planets, then most of the children will be males. The birth will be of daughters if the said house or its lord be in a female sign, or be associated with or aspected by female planets. The number of issues should be determined by a consideration of planets in the house, or those that are posited along with the lord of the 5th house, as to how many of them are in friendly, inimical or depression Navamsas. The number of Navamsas, gained by Jupiter or lord of the 5th indicates the number of issues to be born. Birth of children may occur during the Dasa or Bhukti of Jupiter, or lord of the 5th (from the Ascendant or from the Moon) or planets in or aspecting the 5th.

Example:

Rahu	Mars	Venus Sat.	Sun		Sun		Sat.
	Born 6-7-1914 at 5-34 p.m. Ahmedabad RASI		Merc. Moon	Ketu Venus Ascdt.	NAVAMSA		
				Moon			Rahu
Jupiter	Ascdt.		Ketu		Merc.	Mars Jupit.	

Wife

Karaka for the 7th, Venus is in the 7th, hence bad. He is in conjunction with the lord of the 3rd. The 7th house, the 7th lord and Kalatra-karaka (Venus) are all hemmed in between Mars and the Sun. Considered from the Moon also, the dispositions are highly unfavourable. Hence the native's marriage has been most unsatisfactory. The couple are practically divorced. The lords of the Ascendant and the 7th are very near each other. Marriage took place in the 15th year of the native, Venus is in the second Navamsa. Hence more than one marriage is clearly indicated.

Children

The lord of the 5th is in conjunction with Venus, a Yogakaraka and the Sun, lord of the 7th. Jupiter lord of the 2nd (and also Putrakaraka) is exalted. The 5th is aspected by the Moon. Hence children are indicated. Mercury, the lord of the 5th, has gained seven Navamsas. Birth of seven children is denoted, out of which surviving will be five or six as two malefics intervene in between Aries and Libra in the Navamsa diagram.

		Mars		Mars Jupiter Ascdt.	Sat. Ketu	Venus	
Lagna Rahu	19-8-1886 at Gh. 33-40 RASI		Jupiter			NAVAMSA	
			Sun Venus Mercury Ketu				
Moon		Sat.				Sun Moon Mercruy Rahu	

CHAPTER - X
Timing Events

HINDU Astrology has achieved remarkable success in the matter of timing events, as to when the different indications of the horoscope-marriage, birth and death of children, death of parents, financial gains and losses, access to wealth, loss of reputation, increase of fame and many other events occurring in our daily lives, would fructify or happen. Hindu Predictive Astrology enables one to time and predict events with considerable accuracy. In this book however we shall give the merest outlines, so that readers are given an insight into the vexed question of timing events. It is not in the province of our discussion to investigate into the rationale of the Dasa System but our task consists in giving a faithful account of what in our humble opinion has a sound basis in actual practice and can be relied upon safely. There are any number of Dasas in vogue in India but we propose to deal with Vimshottari or Udu Dasa. In the choice of any particular type of Dasa, the guiding factor should be experience. Vimshottari, in our humble opinion, has been built upon a firm foundation. Some of the recent writers on Astrology reject this system simply because, according to their views, which obviously seem ill-conceived, the system under dis. cussion has no "scientific basis". In their over-enthusiasm to modernise Hindu Astrology, they forget the value of experience which should of course be the true criterion of all knowledge.

In this system there are nine main periods, each presided over by a planet. In the following table will be found the years 'enjoyed' by each planet as well as the constellations corresponding to the period.

Table of Dasas

Aries ♈	Leo ♌	Sagittarius ♐		
4 Aswini	4 Makha	4 Moola	Ketu	7 yrs
4 Bharani	4 Pubbha	4 Poorvashadha	Venus	20 yrs
1 Krittika	1 Uttara	1 Uttarashadha	Sun	6 yrs
Taurus ♉	**Virgo ♍**	**Capricorn ♑**		
3 Krittika	3 Uttara	2 Uttarashadha	Sun	6 yrs
4 Rohini	4 Hasta	4 Sravana	Moon	10 yrs
2 Mrigasira	2 Chitta	2 Dhanishta	Mars	7 yrs
Gemini ♊	**Libra ♎**	**Aquarius ♒**		
2 Mrigasira	2 Chitta	2 Dhanishta	Mars	7 yrs
4 Aridra	4 Swati	4 Satabhisha	Rahu	18 yrs
3 Punarvasu	3 Visakha	3 Poorvabhadra	Jupiter	16 yrs
Cancer ♋	**Scorpion ♏**	**Pisces ♓**		
1 Punarvasu	1 Viskaha	1 Poorvabhadra	Jupiter	16 yrs
4 Pushyami	4 Anuradha	4 Uttarabhadra	Saturn	19 yrs
4 Aslesha	4 Jyestha	4 Revati	Mercruy	17 yrs

Each of the main periods is divided into similar sub-periods (Bhuktis) and each sub-period is divided similarly into inter-periods (Antara). The Antaras are again subdivided into Antarantaras and so on till Swara or the period necessary for the inhaling and exhaling of breath is reached. Nevertheless for all practical purposes the sub-period will be found to be quite sufficient.

In order to calculate the ruling period at birth and date of its commencement it is necessary to obtain the position of the Moon at the time of birth. Every constellation covers 13° 20' of the zodiacal space. To determine the asterism at birth observe the exact longitude of the Moon. In our example horoscope (see page 66) the Moon is in Sagittarius 22° 35'. Reference to the above table will show that in the sign Sagittarius (*) there are four parts (padas) of Moola, four of Poorvashadha and one of Uttarashadha. Each of these parts is 3° 20' in extent. Therefore 4 of Moola=13 degrees 20 minutes; and 22° 35' minus 13 degrees 20 minutes=9 degrees and 15 minutes should be accounted for the Moon as having passed in Poorvashadha at the time of birth. We know that Poorvashadha is ruled by Venus whose period is 20 years. Each asterism being 13 degrees and 20 minutes we must find out what will be the period for 9 degrees and 15 minutes, in Venus Dasa, passed or elapsed.

13 degrees and 20 minutes (800): 9 degrees and 15 minutes (555) :: 20 years 13, months 10 and days 15. This period has expired before birth and from the time of birth only the balance of (yrs, 20 minus yrs. 13, months 10, days 15) yrs. 6-1-15 will go to the benefit of the child. After finding out the Dasa, the sub-period in each of this particular period must be thus determied. Multiply together the number of years of the Dasa period of the planet by the number of years of the Dasa period of the planet whose sub-period is desired. Then cutting off the last figure of the product, multiply it by 3 and keep that figure as days, the other figures in the product will be months. Suppose we want to find the sub-period of Saturn in the major period of Mercury. Saturn's period being 19 years and that of Mercury 17 years, 19x17=323=32 months and 9 days.

We know from the above how to find the unexpired (balance of) Dasa at birth. With the expired portion of Dasa there are certain sub-periods ruling under the period which have also expired. After determining them we can say under what sub-period one's birth has occurred. To do this find all the sub-periods in a period. Add together the Bhuktis from the begining of Janma Dasa (ruling period), one by one, till the total is a little in excess over the expired period of Dasa at birth. Diminish the aggregate by the expired Dasa and the remainder gives the balance of unexpired Bhukti (of the planet in question) at birth.

Example: Required the balance of Bhukti at birth in the case of a person born with a balance of years 6-1-15 in Venus' period (Sukra Dasa).

The Ruling period=Venus 20 years.
Expired period =Yrs. 13-10-15

	Y.	M.	D.
Venus sub-period in Venus' period	3	4	0
Sun's sub-period in Venus' period	1	0	0
Moon's sub-period in Venus' period	1	8	0
Mars's sub-period in Venus' period	1	2	0
Rahu's sub-period in Venus' period	3	0	0
Jupiter's sub-period in Venus' period	2	8	0
Saturn's sub-period in Venus' period	3	2	0
Total	16	0	0

Therefore, yrs. 16 minus yrs. 13-10-15=yrs. 2-1-15, i.e., balance of Saturn's sub-period (Sani Bhukti) in Venus' period (Sukra Dasa) at birth=yrs. 2-1-15.

Judgment

There are several considerations to be taken note of in judging the results of the Dasas and Bhuktis. The general results due to a planet should be carefully weighed and incongruous results, wherever they occur, should be avoided. The relations between the lords of the main period and sub-period should be considered when predicting events during their time. It is certainly difficult to lay down any particular result which will apply to all. Conclusions should be drawn having regard to strength and propensity of the planet. The prediction should always be consistent with the person for whom it is intended, under the condition of life in which he is brought up as well as the physical possibility at the time. As a general proposition it may be stated that a planet during its Dasa generally gives the results pertaining to the houses it rules or aspects. Provided the lord is well placed, that is, in its own sign, exaltation, moolatrikona or friendly house, or conjunction with a yogakaraka or otherwise powerful, it will give rise to good results during its Dasa. Thus when the lord of Lagna is strong, the native will, during the Dasa of the lord of Lagna, have physical happiness and will be happily placed in life. His prosperity will be on the increase. Provided the lord of Lagna is in debilitation and in conjunction with lords of 3, 6 or 11, the native will suffer ailments during the Dasa of the lord of Lagna, will become unhappy and will suffer miseries. Let us take a concrete case. In the adjoining horoscope the results of Jupiter Dasa have to be judged.

Rahu		Moon Saturn	
Lagna	RASI		Sun
			Mars Mercury Venus
	Jupiter		Ketu

Jupiter is the lord of the 2nd and the 11th houses. He is placed in the 10th. Jupiter owning the 2nd is good for wealth. Jupiter here is aspected by Moon (lord of the 6th), Satrun (lord of Lagna and 12) and Mars (lord of 3 and 10). Whilst Jupiter will give, during his Dasa, majority of results pertaining to the 2nd (wealth, family and influence) and the 10th houses (professional advancement, means of livelihood, etc.), he will also produce results due to the 1st, 6th and 3rd houses. Thus the native will amass considerable fortune. There will be considerable professional success. Jupiter being indicator of children, the family will increase. As he occupies the 10th, the native will have some pilgrimage. As the Moon (lord of 6th) and Saturn (lord of Lagna) happen to aspect Jupiter the native is likely to suffer misfortune (of course in the sub-period of Jupiter). The fourth house rules landed properties, education, etc. Jupiter is aspected by the Moon and Saturn from the fourth house. Hence the subject will purchase land and house properties.

From the above-it will be seen that a planet is capable of producing different kinds of results which depend upon ownership, aspect, location and association. Therefore in interpreting results of Dasa and Bhuktis one should exercise very great care in analysing the quality and quantity of effects produced by a planet in the course of its Dasa. The lord of the Dasa has a quality of its own stamped upon it. This will again be modified by the nature of the house, the nature of the aspecting bodies, the favourable and unfavourable situation of the lord of Dasa in Navamsa and other factors. The same argument applies when deciding the results of Bhuktis. In the latter case however the relations and interrelations between the lord (Dasanatha) and the sub-lord (Bhuktinatha) will be the deciding factor. Thus (1) The Dasa periods of the lords of the 6th and the 8th produce harmful results unless they obtain beneficence otherwise. (2) The effects of the ruling planets are intensified at such time as the Sun may be passing through the signs occupied by them or the signs over which they rule. (3) In the course of a Dasa, a planet produces such effects as it indicates by virtue of ownership, association, location and aspect. (4) The Dasa results stand to be modified by the effect of Gochara or transiting planets. (5) The periods of the lord of 5 and 9 are said to give rise to good results. (6) unfavourable results will be realised when the sub-lord and major lord are situated in the 6th and the 8th or the 12th and the 2nd from each other respectively. (7) The general effects of the planets thus related must be taken into account, and their natural relation, as well as their temporary relation in the horoscope must be well considered. Thus the Sun and Venus, although natural enemies, may be respectively in Leo and Libra, in which case they are in temporary good relation occupying the 3rd and the 11th signs respectively from each other. Judgment is made accordingly, but it is to be understood that a temporary friendship will not entirely overcome a radical and constitutional enmity.

During the Dasa of the lord of the 2nd, one can expect success to the family, marrige if not already married, good earnings and generally favourable results. During the Dasa of a planet that is strong and owns the 3rd house one can expect help and co-operation from brothers and other relations, attainment of honour and approbation from others. Help to relations, acquisition of vehicles, land and houses and higher status may be anticipated during the Dasa of the lord of the 4th. Merriment, birth of a son, and general prosperity are likely to result in the Dasa of the 5th house lord. One may predict enjoyment of good health, success over enemies and litigation in the course of the Dasa of the 6th house lord. 7th lord: Marriage if not married, or marital happiness, pleasure trips and family happiness, 8th lord: Discharge of debts, acquisition of amenities and general good. 9th lord Enjoyment of prosperity, birth of grandchildren, happiness and wealth, 10th lord: Professional prosperity, pilgrimage, reputation, respect and realisation of ambitions. 11th lord Influx of wealth, domestic happiness, gains. 12th lord Spending money for good purposes and religious inclination.

The above results hold good provided the planets are strong and favourable. If they are weak and unfavourable, the predictions have to be modified. Thus the lord of the 6th ill-disposed gives rise to diseases, debts and machinations of enemies. Whatever natures, characteristics, diseases, etc., have been mentioned as belonging to the different planets, should be duly assigned to the planets concerned in their respective periods. Rahu and Ketu give effects, good or bad as the case may be, according to the nature of the planet they associate with or the planet in whose house they may be situated.

I give below some of the prominent results by way

of examples that are likely to be produced during different Dasas.

Sun's Period-6 Years

If the Sun is elevated, he displays wisdom, gets money, attains fame and happiness; the Sun in good position, in own house or joined with lord of 9 or 10-happiness, gains, riches, honours; the Sun with lord of 5-birth of children. The Sun when related to lord of 2-becomes rich, earns money, secures property, gains, favours from influential persons. The Sun when debilitated or occupies the 6th or the 8th house or in conjunction with evil planets-contracts evil diseases, loss of wealth, suffers from reverses in employment, penalty and beconies ill.

The Dasa of the Sun in deep exaltation: Sudden gains in cattle and wealth, much travelling in eastern countries, residence in foreign countries, quarrels among friends and relations, pleasure trips and picnic parties and lovely women. *Moolatrikona*: Birth of children, much respect from high personages, gains in cattle and money, acquisition of power and political success. *Leo*: Respect from kings and noble personages, righteous conduct, birth of children and respect among children. *Libra*: Reduced to poverty, always troubled by enemies, failure in undertakings, death of brothers and friends and miserable and complicated life. *Aquarius*: Mental worries, death of wife, loss of property and wealth. The Sun in conjunction with the lord of Lagna gives good gain in the latter half of the Dasa, pleasant functions, vehicles, travelling and respect. The Sun in the 2nd or 7th: Accidents, illness, and other bad results.

Moon's Period-10 Years

The Moon in Ascendant Gets riches and happiness, secures reputation. *In friend's house*: Earns well, learns, and becomes successful. *In enemy's house*: Unfriendly, vexed by family, loss of money in disputes, *With an exalted planet:* Contented and happy. *Evil planet:* Suffers loss from fire, stealing and judicial orders. *With good planet:* Happy and successful, *Moon in the 2nd house:* Increase in family and addition of riches. *In 3rd house:* Happiness to self and brothers, good earning. *In 4th house:* Death of mother if afflicted, earns by cultivation, and attains good name. *In 5th house:* Gets children. *In 6th house:* Becomes unhappy, and gets into litigation. *In 7th house:* Marries if not already married, mentally worried. *In 9th house:* Happy, wealthy and honoured. *In 10th house:* Easy success and wealth, popularity, becomes trustee of religious institution. *In 11th house* Reputation and friends increase, gets landed properties. *In 12th house* Suffers much. *With Sun:* Quarrels with relatives, loss of parents or possessions. *Taurus:* Increase in fame and name, collection of enormous wealth, mental and physical happiness. *Cancer:* Addition in wealth, success in litigation, unexpected finding of treasure, travels. *Scorpio:* Fear from political heads, destruction of relatives, disappointment in every respect, loss of wealth, liberty and honour at risk and much mental uneasiness. *Neecha* (debilitation): Losses and troubles from various sources and mental worry. *Moolatrikona* Respect from sovereigns, many gains, acquisition of landed property, much happiness and sexual enjoyment.

Mars' Period-7 Years

Mars in enemy's house: Unhappy due to disputes, entails the displeasure of superiors and bodily infirmity. *In friend's:* Acquisition of landed properties. *With debilitated planet:* Good carning and reputation. *Aspected by a good planet:* Happy and good effects. *By evil planets :* Becomes destitute. *In 1st house:* Suffers from thieves and poison. In 2nd house: Favoured by others, secures good position, but suffers from facial or eye disease. *In 3rd house:* Happy respected. *In 4th house:* Loss of position, quarrel and worries. *In 5th house:* Loss of money and children, accident to children. *In 6th house* Quarrels, sorrows, debts and enemies. *In 7th house* Unpleasantness with wife or husband, suffers from urinary or bladder troubles. *In 8th House:* Suffer from boils, loses position, travels, *In 9th house:* Bad to father, runs into danger and losses. *In 10th house:* Dispirited by failure, good and bad results in profession depending on the strength or weakness of Mars. *In 11th house:* Respected, gains and success. *In 12th house:* Loss of fortune and children,

Rahu's Period-18 Years

Rahu in 1st house: Illness, friends and relatives suffer. *In 2nd house:* Deprived of land and riches, gets bad food, financial troubles. *In 3rd house:* Respected, happy with children, wealth, wife and brothers. *In 4th house:* Mother's death or sickness, considerable suffering. *In 5th house:* Mental worries. *In 6th house:* Family suffers from thieves, fire, superiors and other complications. *In 7th house:* Is endangered by reptiles, wife suffers. *In 8th house:* Great danger of losing money, etc. *In 9th house:* Misfortunes, loss of father sickness to him, expenses. *In 10th house:* Religious interest, interest in the occult. *In 11th house:* Good in all matters, favour from superiors. *In 12th house:* Gets disheartened, unexpected lossess.

Rahu will not always produce malefic effects. If he occupies the house of a benefic who in turn is well fortified, then Rahu will certainly produce good results. Taking the example horoscope on page 73 it will be seen that Rahu in the course of his Dasa produced quite auspicious results.

Rahu is in the 2nd house and Jupiter, lord of the 2nd, is in the 10th. Rahu is aspected by Mars from the 7th. Rahu should give the results of Jupiter, who aspects the 4th house. Therefore, the native began and completed his education (4th house) during Rahu's period, got married (Mars aspecting from 7th), got a son (because Jupiter is Putrakaraka), and had beginning of professional career (Jupiter in the 10th). Moreover Rahu's Dasa was the second, the ruling period at birth being that of Mars. Hence predominantly beneficial effects were realised.

Jupiter's Period-16 Years

If Jupiter is in Deep Exaltation: Gains wealth, happiness, royal respect, good reputation. *In Cancer:* Travels for good, but is anxious, generally fortunate. *In Capricorn:* Disheartened, worry, serving others. *In own house:* Birth of sons, success in every undertaking, increase in relations and family members, widespread fame, happiness. *In 1st house:* Good health, access to riches. *In 2nd house* Increased income and honours, family happiness. *In 3rd house:* Good relations with brothers and family members and success in undertakings. *In 4th house:* Respected, access to lands and houses, general happiness. *In 5th house:* Official favours, not quite good to children. *In 6th house:* Redemption from debts, enemies will not succeed. *In 7th house:* Travels and pilgrimages, marriage if not already married. *In 8th house:* Homeless, physical and mental illness, increase of enemies. *In 9th house:* Increase of knowledge, gets riches, children and generally fortunate. *In 10th house:* Happy with family, professional success. *In 11th house* Gain of land, family disputes. *In 12th house:* Suffering and uneasiness.

Saturn's Period-19 Years

This Dasa signifies deficiency of thought, dishonour and loss of wealth. It tends to expose the native to the displeasure of superiors. These results should be predicted when Saturn is unfavourably disposed in the horoscope. *Saturn in Capricorn:* Increase in lands, gain in wealth, friendship with illustrious personages. *In Aquarius* Travelling in western countries, success in litigation, good health. *In Enemy's house* Quarrels, loss of position, displeasure of superiors. *In Friend's house:* Happy in general. *In 1st house:* Becomes physically weak, cerebral complaints and loss of money. *In 2nd house:* Suffering, eye trouble, disfavours from superiors and mental disorder if Saturn is heavily afflicted. *In 3rd house:* Loss of brothers or sickness to them, indifferent, gets money. *In 4th house:* Loss of mother or illness to her, litigation troubles, failure in examination. *In 5th house:* Loss of children, weak in mind, Loss of wealth, trouble from servants. *In 6th house:* Trouble from enemies, serious illness. *In 7th house* Suffers losses, dissolution of partnership if in joint business, wife's health a source of worry. *In 8th house:* Generally unfavourable results. *In 9th house:* Loses parents, breaks in fortune. *In 10th house:* Nature of results depends upon the strength and weakness of Saturn, misunderstandings and quarrels with officials. *In 11th house:* Happiness, gain and generally good. *In 12th house:* Constant worries and danger.

Mercury's Period-17 Years

Mercury if exalted: Good earnings, interest in religion, studies, helping others, getting lands and good name. *If debilitated:* Quarrels, loss in business, reputation at stake. *With benefics:* Much happiness, marriage, birth of children, and good profits in trade. *With malefics:* Loss of reputation, quarrels with friends and relatives, low in the estimate of others. *In Gemini:* Access to intellectual treasures, successful termination of educational career, fame and wealth, happiness from wife and children, marrige ceremonies. *In Virgo:* Favour of royal courts, happy life, undisturbed health, charitable activity and unexpected gains. *In 1st house* Good health, fame, profits, education and reputation. *In 2nd house:* Access to wealth, family happiness and redemption from debts. *In 3rd house:* Auspicious celebrations at home, getting jewels, marriage to a brother or a cousin, and good name. *In 4th house* Securing a new house, but unsuccessful. *In 5th house:* Birth of children, learning, earnings, initiation into secret mantras, happiness, befriends high circles. *In 6th, 8th or 12th house* Suffers from nervous troubles, enemies will multiply, quarrels, invokes Government displeasure, disturbance from residence, mind wavering, dangers from fires and thieves and living in foreign places. *In 7th house* Gets wife, education, meets with new acquaintances and will have good happiness. *In 9th house:* Does great things, religiously inclined. *In 10th house:* Happy, increase of fame. *In 11th house:* Given to charity and trade, earns lands and houses.

Mercury will give rise to bad results if placed in the 6th, the 8th or the 12th from the Lagna.

Ketu's Period-7 Years

Ketu produces favourable results if exalted, otherwise the effects will be undesirable. *When Ketu is in the 1st house:* Gets fever, loses reputation, will have mental worry and suffers from wounds and cuts. *In 2nd house :* Much expenditure, sick at heart, eye trouble, family worries, disturbance from native place. *In 3rd house:* Happy but quarrels with brothers. *In 4th house:* Fear of thieves and fires, troubles to mother, litigation and generally unhappy. *In 5th house:* Spends much, loss of children and father, irreligious. *In 6th house:* Endangered by poison, fire and thieves, good earnings and in general, beneficial results will be produced. *In 7th house:* Suffers mentally and bodily and loses wife and children, quarrels with relatives. *In 8th house:* Sickly, wife becomes ill, unnecessary fear. *In 9th house* Material benefits absent, religious interest revived. *In 10th house:* Gets conveyances, success in litigation. *In 11th house:* Happy in business and brothers, bad time for enemies. *In 12th house:* Illness, travels and generally bad results.

Venus' Period-20 Years

Venus is supposed by many to give always pleasant results while on the other hand all that is evil has been ascribed to Saturn to be realised in his Dasa. This view is rather erroneous. Whether Venus, Saturn or any other planet, the nature of the results always depends upon the natural and temporal dignities or afflictions to which the planets are subject to in the horoscope. No planet can ever produce either good, unmixed with evil or only evils unmixed with good.

When Venus is in Taurus: A life of ease and indulgence, travels to foreign lands, company of beautiful girls, ambition of material life fairly realised, symptoms of venereal troubles, access to lands, houses and conveyances. *Libra:* Royal patronage, reputation, gain of wealth, period of extreme passion. *Exalted:* is lost in revelry, gets riches. *Debilitated:* Agitated. frustrated, family put to great distress. *In friendly house:* Debaucherous life, does good to others, cultivates fine arts. *In Enemy's house:* Sickly, bad for the health of wife and children, quarrels with friends and relatives, much expenditure. *Venus in 1st house :* Bodily happiness, increase of reputation. *In 2nd house:* Spends and earn well, everyone respects the subject. *In 3rd house:* Prosperity to brothers and to native. *In 4th house:* Gains, happiness, lands, vehicles, worships mammon and otherwise happy. *In 5th house:* Gets fame, honours, gold, lands and children, his ambitions will be realised. *In 6th house:* Sickly, troubles from enemies, misunderstandings. *In 7th house:* Good gains, family happiness. *In 8th house:* Venereal troubles, unnecessary travels, eating in others' houses. *In 9th house:* Makes superiors happy and derives benefits from them, generally a good period. *In 10th house* Gets fortune, honours and education, fame, money and new friends. *In 11th house:* Happy in children and wealth, general prosperity. *In 12th house:* Is dispossessed, suffers and goes to foreign lands. There will be unnecessary quarrels.

As already indicated in the beginning of this chapter, the above results are of a general character and they should be adapted in such careful manner that peculiarities obtaining in horoscopes under consideration are under no circumstances omitted or overlooked. The periodic influence, stated above will serve as an outline and the reader after consulting the horoscope will be in the best position to determine the nature of influence which will guide the period.

In the sub-period (Bhukti) the lords will have the same influence as in the periods stated above. In this case, however, the influences of both planets (major lord and sub-lord) are to be compounded as also the relation between them taken into account.

A fuller description of the results of sub-periods is given in my book Hindu Predictive Astrology.

CHAPTER - XI
Horary or Answering Questions

PRASNA or Horary Astrology consists of divination by means of planets. This branch of Astrology will be really useful at it enables us to answer questions arising in everyday life in movements of the profoundest anxiety-when life or fortune may be trembling in the balance. The horary astrologer, without the slightest acquaintance with anatomy, physiology and pathology, can take upon himself to decide when doctors disagree and to diagnose the nature of disease which baffles even the wisest physicians. Horary Astrology can be quickly learned by any person of moderate ability and may be well understood and reduced to constant practice. After considerable experience I have found the rules of Horary Astrology (as expounded in Chappanna and Jinendramala) unfailing. The rules of Horary Astrology, to be presented below in a condensed form, should be carefully applied to events of great importance. Prasna Sastra (Horary Astrology) is so vast that it would be impossible to give all the important rules which enable one to anticipate on the mere basis of the question time, what exactly is in the mind of the querist and how the result would be. For a fuller understanding of the subject, readers are referred to my forthcoming book Prasna or Horary Astrology.

First of all cast a horoscope for the time of the question and place the planets both in Rasi and Navamsa diagrams. Estimate the strength and weakness of the various planets and note the following instructions. Below are given a few of the typical questions and how to answer them.

(1) *Whether an event to occur suddenly will be good or bad?* If the rising sign be Leo, Virgo, Libra, Aquarius, Scorpio or Gemini and the rising lord is beneficial then the event to happen will be fortunate. If other signs than mentioned above are rising and the Ascendant lord is not well disposed then the result will be unfavourable.

(2) *Will my health improve?* If the Ascendant lord is in the 5th or the 9th joined or aspected by benefics and the Ascendant is free from malefic aspects, the health will improve. If the Ascendant lord is in the 6th, the 8th or the 12th afflicted then health will not improve.

(3) *Whether the querent shall become rich?* The lord of the 2nd in conjunction or good aspect with the lord of the 9th. If the 2nd house should be free from the aspect of the 6th, the 8th or the 12th lord the question will be fulfilled. The nature of the rising sign and Navamsa-whether movable, common or fixed-reveals the time of becoming rich. Movable signs denote speedy realisation; common signs indicate early consummation and fixed signs suggest uncertainty-extending to years. As regards the exact period within which an event happens, reference should be made to my Horary Astrology.

(4) *Is it advisable to undertake a certain journey?* If the lord of the Ascendant or the Moon be strong and placed in the 3rd or in reception with the lord of the 3rd., then the journey may be safely undertaken. Otherwise it is not advisable to undertake the journey.

(5) *Will it be advisable to sell or buy a certain property?* If the lord of the Ascendant and that of the 7th are well situated, as also the 4th lord, then the transaction may be done with advantage. If Jupiter or Venus be in the 4th, it will be a profitable investment. If Saturn be there, good will not result to the purchaser or the seller.

(6) *Will it be beneficial to shift from one place to another?* If the 7th house and its lord are well disposed and free from

afflictions, he will do well to move to the new place or house to which he thinks of shifting. Otherwise it is not advisable to shift.

(7) *Will the patient recover from his illness at an early date?* If the lords of the 1st and the 6th are in conjunction, the patient is 'unlikely to recover. If a common sign be in the 6th house, the disease will be of its average duration. If the 6th happens to be a movable sign, the sickness will be short. If the 6th be a fixed sign, the disease will be long and hard to cure.

(8) *Is there any treasure in the ground?* If the 2nd house be Taurus. Libra or Cancer and the Moon and Venus or Mars and Rahu be there, then the chances of securing a treasure trove are remote. If the 4th house be Cancer and Jupiter and the Moon occupy it, the ground contains a treasure trove. If Mars or Rahu is associated with the 4th then the questioner will not get access to the treasure trove though it may be present.

(9) *Whether the child to be born will be male or female?* If the lord of the 5th be in a masculine sign and the 5th be a masculine sign, then birth of a boy is indicated; otherwise, a girl. If 5th lord be associated with or aspected by a masculine planet, it will be a boy.

(10) *Shall I win a prize?* When benefics are in 3, 5, 7 and 11 and when the lord of the 2nd, the 9th and the 11th are strong and free from the effects of the 6th and the 8th lords, you will be successful.

(11) *Whether, the questioner shall marry a certain person. If so, when?* If Saturn be in the 7th house, he will be married within three months from the date of question. If the Moon be in 3, 5, 7 or 11 and is aspected by Jupiter, the Sun and Mercury and if benefics occupy quadrants or trines, he will have marriage very early. The lords of the Ascendant and the 7th must be well disposed between each other.

(12) *Will the stolen article be recovered?* If a powerful benefic occupies the 11th house from the Prasna Lagna (Ascendant at question time) or (and) aspected by Jupiter or Venus, predict speedy recovery of the lost article. If the Ascendant falls in a fixed sign, or in a fixed Navamsa, the article will have been stolen by a near relative. The particular direction towards which the article is removed should be ascertained by the most powerful planet found in quadrants at the time of query. In the absence of planets in quadrants the direction is indicated by the rising sign. In the case of planets the directions will be as follows: Sun-East; Venus-S.E.; Mars-South; Rahu-S.W.; Saturn-West; Moon-N.W.; Mercury-North; Jupiter-N.E.; In the case of signs: Aries -East; Leo and Sagittarius-S.E.; Taurus-South; Virgo and Capricorn-S.W.; Gemini-West; Libra and Aquarius-N.W.; Cancer-North; Scorpio and Pisces-N.E.

The questions, pertaining to each Bhava (house) and how to answer them, have been detailed in my book Prasna or Horary Astrology with numerous examples.

Example: On 24th August 1938 at 5-57 p.m., Bangalore, a question was put to the author by a friend who had lost an article. The following were the planetary positions at the time of query:

Saturn	Ketu			Mars			Sun Rahu
Ascdt. Jupiter	RASI		Moon	Moon Sat.	NAVAMSA		Venus
			Mars Sun Merc.				Merc. Jupiter
		Rahu	Venus	Ketu		Ascdt.	

Lord of the Ascendant is in the 2nd (house of wealth). Rising sign is a fixed one. The powerful aspect of Mars on the Ascendant suggests the nature of the person involved as also the aspect cast on Lagna by Mercury and the Sun. The author gave it as his opinion that, if there was any truth in Horary Astrology, the querent had lost some money, that the person involved was his own employee and that with effort the money would be recovered. The forecast was exactly verified as upon the clue furnished by the author, the person who stole the money was discovered and the money, recovered.

The application, of Horary Astrology to idle questions should be deprecated and it should be applied to affairs of great importance and at times of deep anxiety.

Astrology sank to a low ebb owing to the absurd use made of this branch and it is our earnest desire that Horary Astrology should never become "popular" in that sense. By proper application, Astrology may be put to the greatest utility of mankind.

CHAPTER - XII
Transits or Gochara

IT will be seen in the preparation of a horoscope that planetary positions will be fixeds in their respective longitudes. Though the positions of planets in the horoscope are fixed there is no stoppage of planetary movements. Planets take varying periods for moving from one constellation to another and from one sign to another sign. Such movements give rise to the stimulation of radioactive disintegration which on falling on the individual produces psycho-physical changes in his character, disposition and surroundings. In predicting Gochara results the Moon and the birth constellation play a prominent part. The sign in which the Moon is situated in the birth horoscope is the Janma Rasi. The passage of planets through certain angular positions from the radical Moon is technically termed Gochara. Such transits afford a precise and reliable source of prognostication. The Gochara results should never be interpreted without reference to the ruling period and sub-period. Suppose illness is indicated according to the prevailing Dasa and Bhukti: If, according to Gochara the period is likely to be bad then the illness would be of serious type. The results of the prevailing Dasa and Bhukti should be combined with the effects of Gochara before any predictions are ventured.

Gochara (Transits) records the effects of the changes in the positions and movements of the planets on individual lives for any desired time. To read the combined Gochara influence of the planets at any moment a circle of the zodiac is drawn and the radical Moon's position is marked in it.

Next the positions of all the nine planets are noted and the combined transiting influence is read.

The following results are produced by the different planets while transiting the different signs from Janma Rasi (Radical Moon).

The Sun

The Sun, transiting through the sign occupied by the Moon (at birth), signifies change of place; in the 2nd house, loss of wealth; in the 3rd, advent of money and success; in the 4th, portends dishonour; in the 5th, sorrow, ill-health and embarrassment; in the 6th, causes ruin to foes; in the 7th, travelling and ill-health; in the 8th, quarrels and unpleasantness; in the 9th, humiliation and separation; in the 10th, success in undertaking; in the 11th, honour, health and earnings; and in the 12th, quarrels and pecuniary loss.

The Moon

The Moon transiting the 12 houses from her radical position signifies the following results :1) Good disposition and food, 2) expenditure, 3) gain of money, 4) accidents or ill-health, 5) unpleasantness, 6) auspicious results, 7) friendship and gains, 8) trouble and expenses, 9) intimidation and worry, 10) gains and well-being, 11) happiness and pecuniary gain and 12) misery and loss.

Mars

1) Sorrow and accidents, 2) loss and expenses, 3) pecuniary gain and pleasure, 4) trouble from foes, 5) loss of money and illness to children, 6) gain of money, 7) quarrelling, fatigue, accident to wife, 8) fear and danger, 9) indisposition and expenses, 10) change and sorrow, 11) acquisition of money and peace of mind and 12) disease and falls from elevations.

Mercury

1) Trouble and servitude, 2) gain of money, 3) ill-luck, 4) good fortune, 5) poverty and loss, 6) success, 7) illness and vice, 8) pleasure and auspicious events, 9) misery and worry, 10) comfort, 11) happiness and profit, and 12) expenses and misunderstandings.

Jupiter

1) Travelling and fear, rewards, 2) profits and gain of money, 3) obstacles, ill-health, 4) loss of money expenses, 5) happiness, birth of children and pleasure, 6) grief and misery, 7) good health and and fortune, 8) danger and dissatisfaction, 9) access to wealth and risk of losing position and reputation, 10) separation, loss of health and wealth, 11) profit and success in undertakings, 12) affiction and unexpected troubles and mental worry.

Venus

1) Good health and pleasure, 2) gain of money and good luck in general, 3) happiness and pleasant associations, 4) pecuniary gain, 5) happiness and birth of a son, 6) fear of foes and unexpected expenses, 7) worry, grief and quarrels with wife, 8) good income, 9) gain of money, apparel and friends, 10) indisposition and scandal, 11) pleasure and profit and 12) good finance and peace of mind.

Saturn

1) Danger and loss of money, 2) sorrow and accidents, 3) gain and prosperity, 4) expenses, sickness and worry, 5) grief and trouble, 6) happiness and access to property. 7) mental and physical affliction and great suffering, 8) fear, bad reputation and worry, 9) loss of money, ill-health and misfortune, 10) loss of wealth, 11) cruelty and access to money, and 12) danger, worry and financial strain.

Note:-Regarding Saturn, his transit in the 12th, the 1st and the 2nd from the radical Moon has special significance as it goes under the technical name of Sade Sati (7½ years' Saturn) as, to pass through the signs, in his usual course it takes 7½ years. This particular period is dreaded by many as highly malefic; unless the ruling period is powerful, the subject of the horoscope is bound to suffer unexpected miseries. The results produced during Saturn's transit through the 12th, the 1st and the 2nd houses may be summarised thus:-Quarrels and misunderstandings, implication, entanglement in litigation, failure of business, restlessness of mind, change of place, sickness among family members, death of children and mental worry One having good longevity can come under the sway of "7.5% years' Saturn" thrice in his lifetime. During the first time most of the above results will manifest; the second time, no evil results will occur while during the third time the death of the native is invariably caused, unless ruling Dasa does not warrant death.

Rahu and Ketu

1) Sickness and fear, 2) loss of wealth, quarrelling and misunderstandings, 3) happiness and good finances, 4) sickness, danger and sorrow, 5) financial loss and worry, 6) pleasure and happiness, 7) loss and fear, 8) danger to life, 9) quarrelling, mental worry and loss, 10) enmity, 11) happiness and acquisition of money, and 12) expenses and danger.

There are exceptions under which certain planets said to produce malefic effect while transiting certain house, do not manifest anything unfavourable at all. Timing events according to transits in the light of the Ashtakavarga has been enumerated in my book The Ashtakavarga System of Prediction.

Mars and the Sun produce effects during their transit when they are in the first 10 degrees of a sign. Jupiter and

Venus become effective when they are in the 2nd ten degrees while Rahu produces results throughout the entire sign.

Of the different planets, the transiting effects of the slow moving ones, viz., Jupiter, Saturn and Rahu are universally held to be most powerful. The triennial influence may be read from Saturn, the yearly influence from Jupiter, the monthly influence from the Sun and Mercury, and the daily influence from the Moon. For ready reference the benefic and malefic positions of planets are given in the following table:

Planet	Benefic Sign	Malefic Signs
Sun's	3, 6, 10, 11	1, 2, 4, 5, 7, 8, 9, 12
Moon's	1, 3, 6, 7, 10, 11	2, 4, 5, 8, 9, 12
Mars	3, 6, 11	1, 2, 4, 5, 7, 8, 9, 10, 12
Maercury	2, 4, 6, 8, 10, 11	1, 3, 5, 7, 9, 12
Jupiter	2, 5, 7, 9, 11	1, 3, 4, 6, 8, 10, 12
Venus	1, 2, 3, 4, 5, 8, 9, 11, 12	6, 7, 10
Saturn	3, 6, 11	1, 2, 4, 5, 7, 8, 9, 10, 12
Rahu	3, 6, 11	1, 2, 4, 5, 7, 8, 9, 10, 12
Ketu	3, 6, 11	1, 2, 4, 5, 7, 8, 9, 10, 12

APPENDIX - I
Ayanamsa Determination

THERE are two systems of Astrology in India-namely, the Nirayana and the Sayana. The former traces observations of planets to a fixed zodiac, while the latter considers the moving zodiac commencing from the shifting vernal equinox It is certain that the greatest Hindu Astrological writers referred to the fixed zodiac for predictions. And this fact is borne out by experience.

The increment between the beginning of the "fixed' and the "movable" zodiacs or the Nirayana and Sayana positions is referred to as Ayanamsa which increases about 50-1/3 seconds of arc every year. Western Astrology is based upon the Sayana system so that it considers the moving zodiac commencing from the shifting Vernal Equinox. If we deduct this Ayanamsa from the positions of the planets and the cusps of the houses obtained according to the Western system we arrive at the Hindu positions.

When exactly the two zodiacs were in the first point is doubted by a number of astronomers and accordingly the Ayanamsa-precessional distance-varies from 19 to 23°. I do not wish to enter into explaining the complicated processes of astronomy at length which centre attention on the discussion of the exact nature of Ayanamsa but will merely confine myself to giving a suitable and simple methods of determining the Ayanamsa.

First of all, cast the horoscope of birth according to the European system (see Chapter II) and convert it into the terms of the Hindu zodiac by the following process:

1) Subtract 397 from the year of birth (A.D.)
2) Multiply the remainder by 50-1/3 seconds; and reduce the product into degrees, minutes and seconds
3) Substract this result in degrees, minutes and seconds from the cusps of the houses and the planetary positions in the Western figure of birth and the figures obtained will be according to the Hindu system.

Example :

Determine the Ayanamsa for 1935 A.D.
1935-397 = 1538x50" 1/3=77412"
77412"=21° 30' 12"
This is the Ayanamsa for 1935 A.D.

APPENDIX - II

Determination of Ascendant and longitudes of Bhavas according to the Nirayana Tables of Houses by B. V. Raman and R. V. Vaidya.

Example: Born on 2nd November 1935, Saturday, 5-20 a.m. (L.M.T.) Longitude 5 hrs. 10mts. 20 secs. East and Latitude 13 degrees North.

	H.	M.	S.
a) For 1935 (Table I) Y =	18	39	57
b) For 1st November (Table II) =	19	58	34
c) Interval between Mean Noon and birth (L.M.T.) I =	17	20	00
d) Correction at 10 secs, per hour on (C) K =	0	2	53
e) Longitudinal correction between Ujjain and place of birth at 10 secs. per hour (77° 33'-75° 50') C	0	0	1
	56	1	25

Sidereal Times = Y+D-I-K-C.

(I and K are negative since birth is after the noon of 1st November, C is negative since birthplace is to the East of Ujjain).

Sidereal Time 56 h. 1m. 25 s.
Expunging multiples of 24 = 48
Sidereal Time = 8 h. 1 m. 25 s.

Referring to the Tables of Houses for 13° N, the latitude of the place of birth, the nearest sidereal time given is 8 hours.

For this time note down the cusps or longitudes or Bhava Madhyas given along the row for sidereal time 8th. 00m.

10	11	12	Ascendant
6 C 19	6 L 49	7 V 19	7 Li 50

Apply the cusp correction + 0° 6' 28" for 1935 (Table III) to each of the cusps. We get the cusps of the houses to be

10	11	12	Ascendant
6° C 25' 22"	6° L 55' 28"	7° 25' 28"	7° Li 55' 28"